The Language
of **Learning**

Compiled and Edited by
Phylise Banner
and
Dawn J. Mahoney

XML
PRESS

**The Content
Wrangler**
Content Strategy Series

The Language of Learning

Credits

Series Producer:	Scott Abel
Series Cover Designer:	Marc Posch
Publishing Advisor:	Don Day
Publisher:	Richard Hamilton

Disclaimer

Trademarks

XML Press
Denver, Colorado
https://xmlpress.net

First Edition
ISBN: 978-1-937434-84-7 (print)
ISBN: 978-1-937434-85-4 (ebook)

Table of Contents

Foreword

When I first joined *Training* magazine as editor-in-chief in 2007, I knew nothing about the learning and development (L&D) industry, aside from the fact that click-and-repeat online compliance training modules were an instant cure for insomnia. Confronted by an alphabet soup of acronyms—LMS, ADDIE, AR/VR, LEM, LX, GBL, etc.—I quickly realized I had a lot to learn.

This was hammered home by some advice from my predecessor: "Always spell out every acronym and define every term in every article. Never assume the reader has a deep background in training. Otherwise, you will swiftly receive a Letter to the Editor as a reminder."

And I did, despite my best efforts. Boy, do I wish I had a resource tool like *The Language of Learning* to guide me through my initial immersion in all things learning and training! Full disclosure: authors Phylise Banner and Dawn Mahoney have written columns for *Training* magazine over the years, so I know well their high level of expertise and their deep love of learning.

Tapping into their wide-ranging circles of L&D contacts, Dawn and Phylise have collected definitions of learning terms and perspectives from a variety of well-known industry experts that will prove valuable to training newbies, seasoned veterans, business professionals dipping their toes into the industry, and everyone in between.

Even better, they share bios and contact information for those experts, so readers can access additional resources and deeper dives into the five categories and 52 terms covered in the book.

But to my mind, the $64,000 question the book successfully addresses for each term—and what sets this book apart from other similar resources—is: "Why?" Why is it important and why do business and L&D professionals need to know it?

That "why" piece is critical for learner engagement, but sometimes I think we forget how equally crucial it is for those facilitating the learning as they weigh the pros and cons of all the available delivery, content, and evaluation options out there today.

The learning industry has changed dramatically. The COVID-19 pandemic introduced the necessity for nearly all people to learn remotely.

That has spurred organizations to move quickly and agilely to learning methods and technologies they might never have considered before.

Perusing the following pages can help ensure learning and business professionals are all speaking the same language when it comes to delivering effective, engaging, and long-lasting learning. That's one outcome that should never get lost in translation!

Lorri Freifeld
Editor/Publisher
Training magazine

About Lorri Freifeld

Lorri Freifeld has been with Lakewood Media Group's Training magazine since 2007 and currently serves as the editor/publisher. She writes on a number of topics, including talent management, training technology, and leadership development. She spearheads two awards programs: the Training APEX Awards and the Emerging Training Leaders Awards. A writer/editor for the last 29 years, she has held editing positions at a variety of publications and holds a master's degree in journalism from New York University.

Preface

As experienced professionals in the world of learning, we often come across words or phrases that can be interpreted in different ways, depending on the roles we play in designing, developing, delivering, facilitating, or evaluating learning. With the hope of guiding that interpretation, we are pleased to share this compilation book, *The Language of Learning*.

To compile this book, we reached out to our colleagues and friends from a variety of different learning-related careers and invited them to share their expertise. They are educators, designers, developers, technologists, researchers, facilitators, leaders, and mentors—all committed to making significant impacts in the learning space.

We asked our colleagues to select a term, share their definition of that term, explain the importance of the term, and explain why a business professional should know the meaning of the term.

The terms in this book are divided into five categories:

- **Design:** inputs that guide the decisions we make, enabling us to craft meaningful learning experiences.
- **Strategy:** philosophies that inform actions that we take to set and reach established learning goals and outcomes.
- **Implementation:** approaches we take to transform learning designs into tangible, measurable learning experiences.
- **Evaluation:** methodologies we use to test the validity of our work and determine what needs to be fixed or improved.
- **Innovation:** products, applications, and tools that have a notable impact on the future landscape of learning.

As with most disciplines, the language of learning includes unique terms and jargon. To that end, we have also included a glossary of terms to serve as a reference as you explore this book.

Our hope is that these definitions, the explanations, and the resources associated with each term in this book enable you to ask more informed questions, enhance the work that you are doing, and inspire further exploration of the learning landscape.

We wish you well on this learning journey!

Dedication

This book is dedicated to mentor and friend, Karen Swan, who died suddenly and peacefully on September 5, 2021. In loving memory, we will always be big chickens.

Design

The process of design is about making choices. Some of those choices are informed and others are intuitive.

Scholars argue whether the process of design should be considered art or science. In the realm of learning, we posit that the process of design is a craft—one honed through the practice of making decisions and creatively shaping the results of those decisions.

The terms in this book that fall under the category of design guide the high-level decisions we make about learning, and provide a foundation for building an understanding of education that helps business professionals collaborate with education professionals to create effective learning experiences that meet their organization's needs.

Terms in this section:

- Accessibility
- Andragogy
- Bloom's Taxonomy
- eLearning
- Gamification
- Heutagogy
- Instructional Design
- Learner Preference
- Learning Environment Modeling
- Learning Experience Design
- Microlearning
- Pedagogy
- Personalized Learning

Char James-Tanny
Accessibility

What is it?

The extent to which content is available, understandable, and usable by all, regardless of disabilities or impairments such as sensory, physical, cognitive, intellectual, or situational.

Why is it important?

Accessibility equals usability for (almost) everyone. If people with disabilities (PWD) cannot use your product, they might not tell you, but they will tell everyone they know. They'll also compare it to a competitor's product that *is* accessible. Many countries have mandated that products and their documentation must be accessible. Some, like the United States, require it on government websites, for companies doing business with the federal government, or public access. Others require it for everything.

About Char James-Tanny

Char James-Tanny works in technical publications at Schneider Electric. She has over 40 years of experience as a technical communicator. She has spoken around the world about accessibility, social media, web standards, collaboration, and technology. Char is currently involved in the accessibility initiative at Schneider Electric, helping various teams make their products more accessible for employees and customers. In addition to the links shown below, Char can also be found on Mastodon (@charjtf@a11y.info) and Spoutible (@charjtf).

Email charjtf@gmail.com
LinkedIn linkedin.com/in/charjtf
Facebook facebook.com/CharJTF

Why does a business professional need to know this?

If your content, product, or building isn't accessible, you're ignoring as much as 25% of your audience[4]. And that audience, globally, is exceptionally loyal and has disposable income of close to $2 trillion USD[5]. Additionally, making your product more accessible helps everyone, not just people with disabilities, which makes it more marketable.

Incorporating accessibility can be daunting at first. It helps if accessibility is incorporated during design (and it costs less than trying to retrofit or remediate later in the process). It also helps to include people with disabilities during all phases.

Even if you're starting after product design has begun or is completed, you may still incorporate aspects of accessibility to make your products usable by people with:

- **Sensory disabilities:** sight, hearing, and more
- **Mobility and physical disabilities:** need assistance while walking, can't use a mouse, and so on caused by an accident, disease, or disorder
- **Neurological disorders:** ADD, ADHD, cerebral palsy, dementia, learning (dyslexia), muscular dystrophy, and more
- **Intellectual disorders:** diminished cognitive development
- **Invisible disabilities:** chronic pain, arthritis, diabetes, sleep disorders, and more

Things to consider:

- *Color contrast ratio*: test to ensure that text can be read in bright light and by people who are colorblind.
- *Alt text:* add to images, and create transcripts for videos.
- *Semantic markup:* apply to help those using *screen readers* (assistive technology that reads documents) and people with intellectual disabilities.
- **Tab order:** verify that it is logical (press TAB to move through the page). This helps screen-reader users, those with cognitive issues, and those who do not use a mouse.

These items often help people without disabilities, too.

Alexandra Pickett
Andragogy

What is it?
The theory and practice of supporting self-directed learners, typically, but not exclusively, adult learners.

Why is it important?
Learning is best when it is directed, supported, facilitated, guided, and designed to be appropriate to the context of the individual learner.

About Alexandra Pickett
Alexandra M. Pickett gives leadership and direction to SUNY (State University of New York) Online Teaching. She is the former director of the Open SUNY Center for Online Teaching Excellence, and the former associate director of the award-winning SUNY Learning Network. Working with 64 SUNY institutions, she has directly supported or co-ordinated the development of over 6,000 online faculty and their online courses. She has also taught *Introduction to Online Teaching* in the Curriculum Development and Instructional Technology (CDIT) master's program at the University at Albany.

Email Alexandra.Pickett@suny.edu
Website online.suny.edu/onlineteaching/meet-the-team/alex/
LinkedIn linkedin.com/in/alexandrapickett/

Why does a business professional need to know this?

The term *andragogy*, which most often refers to the theory and practice of supporting adult learners, was coined by German educator Alexander Kapp in 1833 and popularized by American educator Malcolm Knowles in the 1970s[16].

Andragogy is situated on the learning continuum between *pedagogy*, where what is learned and how it is learned is teacher-determined and directed, and *heutagogy*, where what is learned and how it is learned is determined solely by the learner. In andragogy what is learned is determined by the teacher, and how it is learned is directed by the learner[14].

Understanding the learner's role in learning is essential to effectively, efficiently, and successfully designing learning. The learning content must be appropriate to the context, and position on the continuum, of the individual learner. And it is not necessarily dictated by age or stage of development of the learner.

There are several key principles that differentiate andragogy:

- **Role**: the instructor functions more as a guide on the side, rather than as a sage on the stage. Learners want choices and options and consider themselves equal partners in the learning process.
- **Environment**: collaborative and less formal.
- **Learning**: learner-centered and experiential in nature, taking life experiences and prior knowledge into account, rather than being *didactic* and focused on knowledge acquisition or content-oriented.
- **Methods**: deeper learning and engagement methods, include problem-solving, case studies, role-playing, simulations, project-based activities, self/peer evaluation, and group or paired activities.
- **Curriculum**: designed to support applied learning and experience (including mistakes) that is practical and immediately relevant to the learner, i.e., what the learner needs/wants to know, rather than a standardized curriculum determined by society and/or educators.
- **Motivation**: Rather than being driven by external pressures to learn, the drive to learn is directed and sustained by the learner's own internal motivation. Learners assume active responsibility for their learning.

Joy Adams
Bloom's Taxonomy

What is it?

A hierarchical model that classifies the cognitive processes of learning into increasing levels of complexity and abstraction. Bloom's Taxonomy was proposed in 1956 by a team led by educational psychologist Benjamin Bloom.

Why is it important?

Bloom's taxonomy remains highly influential as a framework for scaffolding instruction and articulating learning objectives. Often depicted as a pyramid[31], it represents a progression from lower-order to higher-order thinking skills:

1. **Remember:** Recall facts or basic knowledge
2. **Understand:** Explain ideas or concepts
3. **Apply:** Use knowledge to address novel contexts
4. **Analyze:** Make connections among ideas
5. **Evaluate:** Exercise judgment and defend decisions
6. **Create:** Develop new or original work

About Joy Adams

Joy K. Adams, PhD, is an e-learning instructional designer and adjunct instructor of geography with 25 years of experience in higher education. Her specializations include Universal Design for Learning, digital accessibility, faculty development and training, inclusive pedagogy, and active/applied learning.

Email   joy.adams@gmail.com
Website   elevatedlearningdesignllc.com
LinkedIn   linkedin.com/in/joykadamsphd/

Why does a business professional need to know this?

Bloom's Taxonomy informs the development of effective employee and consumer-facing training programs by helping facilitators to:

Identify the type(s) of knowledge required: The taxonomy divides knowledge into four domains: factual, conceptual, procedural, and metacognitive. Understanding the types of knowledge a training program seeks to impart informs the development of relevant content and instructional strategies.

Target the appropriate level of learning for a given audience: Lower-order cognitive skills are prerequisites for the development of higher-order skills. For example, learners must first be able to recall and understand industry terminology before they can correctly apply those terms in written and verbal communication.

Articulate the desired outcomes of a training program: Various sources have mapped action verbs[34] to each level of Bloom's taxonomy to support the development of learning outcomes that are well-aligned with instructional goals. Clear outcomes ensure learners understand the purpose of the training and how it will help them perform specific tasks, which can boost engagement and persistence. By first articulating the tasks and behaviors a training program will address, instructors can design relevant activities and assessments, making the training experience more efficient and effective.

Allocate time and resources for training: More complex cognitive tasks require more time for instruction, more opportunities for practice, and more robust support for learners.

Evaluate training: By considering the level of learning and intended outcomes of training programs, evaluation instruments can more accurately assess their effectiveness and return on investment.

Joe Ganci
eLearning

What is it?

Any form of learning through electronic media, such as the internet, web apps, or other means. The most effective eLearning is almost always highly interactive, challenging, and engaging.

Why is it important?

Too often, eLearning content is thrown together without much thought as to how effective it might be for the learners. It is no longer enough to place a PowerPoint deck with narration online and then quiz learners. Instead, effective eLearning uses an individualized approach that challenges learners to solve real work-related problems. It also presents a consistent message to all learners. And when done well, it is both economical and an effective use of resources.

About Joe Ganci

Joe Ganci leads eLearningJoe, LLC, a custom learning company. He has been involved in every aspect of multimedia and learning development. Joe holds a computer science degree, and he writes books, research papers, and articles about eLearning. He is an award-winning eLearning guru, and he consults with clients and delivers keynotes and classes worldwide. His mission is to increase employee productivity with engaging eLearning experiences that really work.

Email	joe@elearningjoe.com
Website	elearningjoe.com
Twitter	@elearningjoe
LinkedIn	linkedin.com/in/elearningjoellc/

Why does a business professional need to know this?

Every successful business strives for constant improvement and growth. Training is an important part of achieving those goals. eLearning, while important, is not a panacea for every training need. At times it makes more sense to hold training in a meeting room. At other times it may be better to watch a training video.

What does eLearning provide? When it is done well, eLearning delivers an individualized experience to each learner, one that molds itself automatically to each learner's needs. Someone who is already proficient in the content need not be bored; those who are new to the content need not be overwhelmed. Learners should be challenged at an appropriate level so they can solve real-life problems that they encounter in the workplace.

Well-designed eLearning starts learners out with the same set of challenges, using case scenarios and similar approaches. And it aims to bring all learners to the same level of proficiency. However, it allows more experienced learners to progress quickly, and for those who struggle, it gives extra time and levels to ensure a complete grasp of the material.

This process does not require a lot of money to create, but it does require expertise in creating eLearning. Just as you wouldn't hire someone who has never popped the hood of a car to fix an engine problem, you want to make sure that eLearning expertise is brought to bear to ensure money and time are not wasted and that the learning is effective.

Karl Kapp
Gamification

What is it?

The use of game-based mechanics, dynamics, aesthetics, and *game thinking* to engage people, motivate action, promote learning, and solve problems. Gamification applies gaming principles to more traditional learning methods, in contrast with *game-based learning*, which presents learning content in a game format.

Why is it important?

Gamification is a powerful technique for motivating individuals to engage in a variety of activities, including learning. Popular apps, such as Duolingo (duolingo.com), have successfully applied the techniques of gamification to keep people motivated and learning.

About Karl Kapp

Karl Kapp, EdD, is a professor of Instructional Technology at Commonwealth University in Bloomsburg, PA. He is recognized worldwide as a pioneer in the gamification of learning and is an award-winning international keynote speaker, consultant, and gamification entrepreneur. He is author of over a dozen books including *The Gamification of Learning and Instruction* and a dozen LinkedIn Learning Courses. Karl is founder of The Wisdom Learning Group and consults internationally with Fortune 500 companies, governments, and not-for-profits.

Email	karlkapp@gmail.com
Website	karlkapp.com
Twitter	@kkapp
LinkedIn	linkedin.com/in/karlkapp/
Facebook	facebook.com/gamificationLI/

Why does a business professional need to know this?

Employee and customer engagement is a huge challenge for many organizations. In a distraction-filled economy, it's hard to both attract and maintain attention. Gamification techniques and the process of thinking like a game designer can be helpful in a variety of business contexts, from designing products to educating employees to maintaining customer loyalty.

Correctly applying *game elements* can improve employee *engagement*. You can start with a specific objective in mind, such as reducing quality-control errors or increasing sales, then apply game elements, such as creating meaningful stories, creating points, providing *badges*, creating a leaderboard, and fostering collaboration.

One of the big myths about gamification is that it's about playing games. It is not. It's about using elements from games but not creating an entire game. One of the best ways to sell gamification is to talk about the high level of engagement that gamification encourages. If you can sell that basic idea, you can then run a pilot study to determine the impact of using gamification within your organization.

Don't go all in on gamification until you understand how your corporate culture will react to gamified approaches. No two corporate cultures are the same, so a one-size-fits-all approach won't work. Gamification needs to be carefully planned and executed to be successful.

Bill Pelz
Heutagogy

What is it?
An approach that prepares students for life-long learning by developing autonomous, self-directed learning skills. Learners take an active role in deciding what to learn and how to learn.

Why is it important?
Designing effective learning environments for adults requires an understanding that adults learn differently than children. Heutagogical learning environments take advantage of these differences to give adult students the skills they need to teach themselves.

About Bill Pelz
Bill Pelz is professor of psychology and instructional designer for online learning at Herkimer College / SUNY. As the lead faculty trainer for the SUNY Learning Network from 1999 until 2010, Bill has facilitated the development of over 2500 online college courses. Awards include the SUNY Chancellor's Award for Excellence in Teaching, the Sloan Consortium Award for Excellence in Online Teaching, and the SUNY Chancellor's Award for Excellence in Scholarship and Creative Activities.

Email	pelzwe@herkimer.edu
Website	herkimer.edu/learn/online-learning/
LinkedIn	linkedin.com/in/bill-pelz-5642a147/
Facebook	facebook.com/bill.pelz

Why does a business professional need to know this?

Heutagogy is also referred to as self-determined learning and seeks for learners to develop a sense of autonomy over their own learning.

Think of learners as consumers of knowledge. Heutagogy empowers learners to consume knowledge on their own terms. Learners decide what to learn, when to learn, how fast, how much, with whom, and from whom.

Heutagogy encompasses and extends prior adult-focused learning strategies, such as learner-centered learning, *andragogy*, and others. A similar philosophy is expressed in the term *autodidactic learner* which implies a preference for learning without external incentives.

Traditional educational practices such as drills, lectures, and memorization weaken our propensity to learn. In the worst case, the love of learning can be extinguished. A business professional needs to recognize that the audience for a course or other training has probably experienced a lifetime of traditional education and may have lost interest in learning. A heutagogical learning environment that empowers learners can help rekindle curiosity and a love of learning, leading to more effective learning.

Dawn Mahoney
Instructional Design

What is it?

The crafting of learning content that responds to the needs of the business and creates learning experiences that make it possible for learners to acquire the new knowledge and skills they need to be effective in their work.

Why is it important?

Too much learning content is created by simply throwing together a handout or slide deck. Instructional design applies educational knowledge and expertise to bring the most effective content to learners. Good instructional design helps you discern what learners need to know and how to create content that meets those needs.

About Dawn Mahoney

Dawn J. Mahoney CPTD (Certified Professional in Talent Development) is passionate about developing better learning content, better learning strategy, and better dialog—all of it to help facilitate people's success. She loves to see the moment when the learning dawns on her learners and they begin to get it. In 2015, Dawn founded Learning In the White Space, which is a boutique consultancy devoted to all of the above. What might you need help with? Contact her today!

Email	dawnjmahoney@gmail.com
Website	dawnjmahoney.com
Twitter	@DawnJMahoney
LinkedIn	linkedin.com/in/dawnjmahoney/
Facebook	facebook.com/LearningInTheWhiteSpaceLLC

Why does a business professional need to know this?

Instructional design provides a structure for creating learning content that helps you avoid creating content that wastes valuable resources and is possibly doomed to fail.

One useful model for instructional design is ADDIE: Analyze, Design, Develop, Implement, and Evaluate. This model can help you align your training program with your business needs and strategy[104]. Here are the steps in the ADDIE model:

Analyze: Uncover needs, including business needs stated by leaders, concerns from subject matter experts, and other staff needs. This should include a review of relevant business performance data and metrics.

Design: Craft a strategy and specifications, including:

- How learners will interact with the content
- What the learner experience will be
- How to structure quizzes and assessments
- How *performance support* will be provided
- How to evaluate whether the strategy worked

Develop: The point at which planning and strategy come to life, and the training deliverables are created.

Implement: Learners begin experiencing the content and you can begin collecting data for evaluation and updates.

Evaluate: As the learning content is completed, so is the evaluation plan. Evaluation focuses on the course, not the learners, and includes:

- What gets evaluated
- What is the timeframe for evaluation
- How does learner progress compare to business expectations

This is just a brief glimpse into instructional design. Hopefully, it provides context, helps you hire instructional design professionals, and helps you work with professionals to create effective learning content.

Cindy Plunkett
Learner Preference

What is it?
Every learner has preferred ways to learn; *preference* meaning liking one alternative over another for how knowledge or skills are acquired.

Why is it important?
Every learner brings with them their own interests, needs, and experiences, which influence their preferences for how to learn. By acknowledging and addressing learner preferences you can offer more equitable access to knowledge and skills, which helps remove barriers to learning, increase learner enthusiasm, and make it more likely that learners will successfully complete a course.

About Cindy Plunkett
Cindy Plunkett is a seasoned expert in learning and development with more than 20 years experience in instructional design, development, and project management. She is the Canadian eLearning Conference executive director, part-time professor at Ontario Tech University, and co-creator of the Educational Technology for Health Practitioner Education curriculum at the University of Toronto. Cindy has a masters in educational technologies from the University of British Columbia and a PhD in education from Northcentral University. Cindy has experience speaking and facilitating nationally and internationally.

Email   sensei.cindy.plunkett@gmail.com
Twitter   @DrSenseiCindy
LinkedIn   linkedin.com/in/cindyplunkett/

Why does a business professional need to know this?

When learning is designed to reduce barriers and address preferences, all learners can participate in inclusive, equitable, and meaningful learning. What will motivate and engage one learner may de-motivate and disengage another. Taking the time to understand your learner's preferences can make a tremendous difference to that person's success.

Learner preference is distinct from *learning style*. That is, while there is evidence that learners' preferences have an impact on how open students are to learning, there is little evidence that a particular style of learning is more effective, regardless of preferences[110][112].

Here are some examples of learner, or learning, preferences:

- Visual (spatial)
- Aural (auditory)
- Verbal (linguistic)
- Physical (kinesthetic)
- Logical (mathematical)
- Social (interpersonal)
- Solitary (intrapersonal)

As a business professional, understanding learner preferences enables you to provide learners with the flexibility to use their preferred learning styles to acquire the knowledge and skills they need to drive your organization's performance and strategy.

Valuing learner preferences as a company and leveraging them to encourage employees to proactively increase their knowledge, skills, and performance can contribute to a high-impact learning culture.

Embracing a variety of methods, materials, and assessments to identify and address learner preferences can give your company a competitive edge and keep your employees' expertise up to date in their field today and in fields that are yet to be discovered.

Bucky Dodd
Learning Environment Modeling (LEM)

What is it?
A visual and collaborative process for designing the spaces and places where people learn.

Why is it important?
Effective communication and collaboration during learning design projects often mean the difference between success and failure. When groups design learning experiences together, ideas and decisions often are invisible and lack a common *design system*.

Learning Environment Modeling (LEM) equips educators and learning experience designers with a visual system for creating, collaborating, and communicating. This helps save time, clarify ideas, and engage people around a shared vision for the learning experience.

About Bucky Dodd
Bucky Dodd, PhD, is the Chief Executive Officer and Principal Consultant at ClearKinetic, a boutique consultancy specializing in creating one-of-a-kind education and training solutions.

Email	BuckyDodd@ClearKinetic.com
Website	clearkinetic.com
Twitter	@buckydodd
LinkedIn	linkedin.com/in/buckydodd

Why does a business professional need to know this?

The learning functions of organizations can sometimes seem like an expense that lacks a connection to business results. Learning environment modeling connects the learning and business functions of organizations by aligning investments in learning environments to results and evidence.

At the core of learning environment modeling is a common design language[123] and a set of standards that allow people from diverse backgrounds and experiences to communicate clearly, effectively, and consistently when planning and designing learning experiences.

The learning environment modeling system comprises visual canvas tools to organize ideas and visual building blocks that visualize the structure and flow of learning experiences. The system can be used in both analog and digital formats and provides a common format for decision making and strategic thinking. The system is most effectively used during collaborative planning and design projects by a skilled and experienced facilitator.

Learning environment modeling gives educators and learning experience designers an effective tool to visualize, communicate, and collaborate on projects and initiatives. This can help you save time, reduce risks, and engage diverse stakeholders in meaningful, efficient, and effective ways.

Jessica Knott
Learning Experience (LX) Design

What is it?

The process of incorporating student-centered design approaches, including *human-centered*, *service design*, and *user-experience design* methods, to design and develop shared learning experiences for students and instructors.

Why is it important?

Whether learning materials are online, face-to-face, or a blend, considering the learners' experience in relation to the goals and outcomes is key to developing successful learning paths. For business professionals, Learning Experience (LX) design is important because it frequently translates to customer success, which leads to higher sales and better customer stories[124].

About Jessica Knott

Jessica Knott, PhD, has been a UX/LX leader for over a decade, spanning the public and private sectors. Her UX work has been featured in education, non-profit, government, and athletics industries.

Email   jlknott@gmail.com
Website   jessknott.com
Twitter   @JLKnott
LinkedIn   linkedin.com/in/jessknott/

Why does a business professional need to know this?

Learning is experienced in different ways by different people, with different goals and learning needs.

User-experience design is defined as the "systematic study of goals, needs, and capabilities of users to specify design, construction, or improvement of tools to benefit how users work and live"[126].

Learning experience design (LX) uses similar methods to design the experiences by which learners work and learn. "Learning experience design is the process of creating learning experiences that enable the learner to achieve the desired learning outcome in a human-centered and goal-oriented way"[127].

LX design methods offer a means for instructors, trainers, instructional designers, curriculum developers, and others to identify learning paths that maximize usability, accessibility, and wayfinding abilities for their students. *Personas, journey maps, prototypes*, and applied user and *usability research* provide a framework for identifying learner needs. They also provide high-impact opportunities for refinement of course design, based on learner needs.

As eLearning becomes an increasingly important strategy, businesses benefit from identifying customers as learners with an eye toward teaching them how best to use products and services.

Academically, LX design provides a means to identify learner needs and design experiences that foster deep learning.

By understanding learners as users, as well as content consumers, you can make design decisions that reduce the *cognitive load* of learners navigating course content.

Karin Rex
Microlearning

What is it?

A snippet of training content that can stand alone, microlearning is streamlined to have a very tight focus on a single, bite-sized concept.

Why is it important?

Learners are busy and their minds are overtaxed. Microlearning can ease their path by offering content in small bursts that are more likely to resonate and stick.

About Karin Rex

As a learning experience architect, Karin Rex saves adult learners from the mind-numbing effects of boring training by hand-crafting rich, engaging learning experiences. Since 1989, Karin has owned Geeky Girl, LLC, where she devotes her time to writing, course development (microlearning, eLearning, instructor-led, blended), and teaching. Karin especially loves facilitating in, and designing for, the virtual classroom because it allows her to connect with a global audience without having to pack a suitcase!

Email   rex@karinrex.com
Website   karinrex.com
LinkedIn   linkedin.com/in/karinrex/

Why does a business professional need to know this?

Highly concentrated training in the form of microlearning helps decrease a learner's *cognitive load* and increases the opportunity for *learning transfer*. While technically not defined by length, microlearning is typically accomplished in five minutes or less and focuses on one terminal learning objective or task. Think of a typical training session as a meal and microlearning as a tasty morsel.

Angela Gunder
Pedagogy

What is it?
The study and science of the development of learning.

Why is it important?
Pedagogy is used to describe the practices, mindsets, and processes related to learning, such as *critical pedagogy* and *open pedagogy*.

Pedagogy is sometimes used to describe how children learn in school. More broadly, it is used to describe prescribed learning content that is closely guided, as opposed to self-directed (*andragogy*) or self-defined (*heutagogy*).

When considering learning as a practice, pedagogy focuses on the ways in which people learn, focusing on the formative, or developing, practices of how people first learn how to learn.

About Angela Gunder
Angela Gunder, PhD, is the Chief Academic Officer for the Online Learning Consortium, where she is responsible for advancing the thought leadership of the OLC. She is an online instructor for The University of Arizona School of Information, teaching courses on instructional design, digital media, web design, and gameful learning. Her research focuses on open remix practices, open culture, digital literacies, narrative digital learning practices, and emerging technology for language acquisition.

Email   angela.gunder@gmail.com
Website   angelagunder.com
LinkedIn   linkedin.com/in/angelagunder/

Why does a business professional need to know this?

A business professional should have at least a basic understanding of what pedagogy is because it affects the *learning strategy* employed in their organization.

Pedagogy shows us how to help learners meet educational goals by using what we know about how people learn. By focusing on our audience first, we take a pedagogical approach that aligns the learner's needs to the content and spaces we design for learning.

Traditionally, pedagogy, or pedagogical approaches, referred to teaching methods selected and applied to learning content. But pedagogy has evolved and expanded to use the results of research on how learners learn to develop training that presents learning content more effectively. Pedagogy has also expanded beyond its focus on K-12 school students to encompass learners of any age.

Other relevant terms that apply to the art and science of learning and learning content design, are *andragogy* (instructors determine and guide decisions as to what content is to be learned and learners shape how they will learn the material) and *heutagogy* (learners determine what and how they will learn with support from an instructor).

Ragini Lall
Personalized Learning

What is it?
A learning approach that focuses on individual learners and their needs, abilities, and interests, with the objective of accelerating their learning.

Why is it important?
Navigating today's volatile, uncertain, ambiguous, and complex world requires everyone to be a life-long learner. In this context, coupled with an increasing emphasis on people's ability to learn, personalized learning prioritizes the individual learner. It differs from traditional approaches that primarily focused on a system's efficiency rather than its effectiveness. Personalized learning should align with the organization's strategic goals and the needs of the individual.

About Ragini Lall
As a learning designer, Ragini Lall combines tools from design thinking, experience design, and curricular design to develop innovative learning solutions. She also worked as an online learning fellow supporting Harvard faculty in transitioning residential courses to online learning during the pandemic. She has earned her EdM in technology, innovation, and education at the Harvard Graduate School of Education.

Email	ragini@thestudentact.com
Website	thestudentact.com
Twitter	@raginilall
LinkedIn	linkedin.com/in/ragini-lall-the-student-act-2202b825/

Why does a business professional need to know this?

While the term has been around for decades, in today's digital age personalized learning has become a much-hyped buzzword. It is hotly debated amongst learning specialists for the oxymoronic impression the words *personal* and *learning* create in direct contrast to the social nature of learning.

However, it is not all hype. Talent development technology increasingly has the potential to deliver targeted, just-in-time learning experiences. This is a game-changer for the success of an organization when learning goals are aligned with the strategic priorities of the business. Moving away from a one-size-fits-all approach to learning allows each person to more quickly acquire the precise skills and knowledge needed to do their job well.

This approach is delivered through custom sequences of learning opportunities packaged via media and designed based on factors such as role, geography, current proficiency, or learners' interests. These media assets are then situated within a virtual learning environment, such as a *learning management system* or a next-generation learning platform, complementing in-person training.

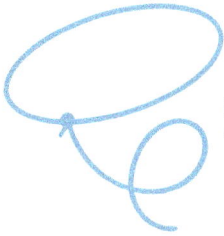

Strategy

Strategy encompasses the resources we use and the actions we take to reach our goals. Strategy defines the landscape and shapes each step in the path from design to implementation. It informs how learning designers, developers, and facilitators allocate resources to ensure that learning experiences are viable, manageable, and sustainable.

The terms in this book that fall under the category of strategy focus on the philosophies that inform the actions we take to set and reach established learning goals and outcomes.

Terms in this section:

- Adaptive Learning
- Behaviorism
- Blended Learning
- Coaching
- Cognitive Load
- Cognitivism
- Communities of Practice
- Competency Based Learning
- Constructivism
- Experiential Learning
- Game-Based Learning
- Interaction
- Learning Ecosystem
- Online Learning
- Open Educational Resources
- Problem-Based Learning
- Scaffolding
- Social and Informal Learning

JD Dillon
Adaptive Learning

What is it?

The purposeful use of data, technology and content to modify a person's learning and support experience to address their proven individual needs.

Why is it important?

Scale is one of the biggest challenges facing modern learning and development (L&D) teams. It doesn't matter if you're a team of one or one thousand. It's almost impossible to meet the changing needs of each individual you support. Unfortunately, this lack of time and resources often results in the delivery of generic, one-size-fits-all training that fails to meet anyone's needs. Adaptive learning helps L&D overcome this obstacle through the strategic blend of modern data and technology practices. Adaptive learning systems adjust the learning experience to focus on each person's timely needs. This may include tactics such as sequencing the delivery of digital content based on a person's profile, reinforcing topics with which a person is struggling and nudging a person towards an additional learning opportunity based on their stated interests or goals.

About JD Dillon

JD Dillon is a veteran talent development leader, former Disney cast member and dedicated Back to the Future aficionado. He became a learning and performance expert over two decades working in operations and talent management with dynamic organizations, including The Walt Disney Company, Kaplan and AMC. A respected international speaker and author of The Modern Learning Ecosystem, JD continues to apply his passion for helping people do their best work every day in his roles as Axonify's Chief Learning Architect and founder of LearnGeek, an insights and advisory practice.

Email   jd@learngeek.co
Website   learngeek.co
Twitter   @JD_Dillon
LinkedIn linkedin.com/in/jddillon/

Why does a business professional need to know this?

Adaptive learning uses tools like *data analytics*, algorithms, and artificial intelligence to present the specific content a learner needs to complete right now, based on what is occurring in the business or on the job.

A fundamental contradiction challenges modern business: agility is essential for maintaining pace with the ever-changing nature of work. Therefore, people must always be learning and developing to meet the present and future needs of the organization. At the same time, these same people are time-starved, feel overworked, and possibly lack the resources they need to do their jobs.

So, to keep the organization moving forward it is incumbent upon learning and development teams to be highly effective in presenting learning content that is economical and efficient. One way to do this is to make adaptive learning methods part of the workplace *learning strategy*. By applying the latest approaches to data, technology, and content, staff receives the learning and development support they need—when and where they need it.

Adaptive learning takes a variety of forms. For example:

- Resource recommendations
- Suggested reading or references
- Coaching guidance
- Targeted reinforcement
- Structured activities, such as challenges, scenarios, simulations.

Adaptive learning not only reduces the time an individual spends, by recognizing and leveraging their existing capabilities, it also adapts the learning experience to the individual. Adaptive learning is designed to identify and close knowledge gaps quickly, promote engagement, and scale development in ways that were previously impossible. Note: adaptive learning might also coincide with learners' preferred method(s) for learning. See *learner preference* and *personalized learning*

Jillian Powers
Behaviorism

What is it?

A theory of learning based on the idea that all sources of behavior are external (in the environment), not internal (in the mind, in the head). Also known as Behavioral Learning Theory.

Why is it important?

Behavioral learning theory shows us how to leverage important factors such as repetition, positive reinforcement, and motivation to achieve better results from the learning initiatives we employ. The biggest advantage of a behavioral approach to learning is that it focuses on observable, *measurable behaviors*, making it useful for modifying behaviors in the real world.

About Jillian Powers

Jillian Powers, PhD, is an assistant professor of instructional technology at Florida Atlantic University (FAU) for the College of Education. She earned her PhD in curriculum and instruction with a specialization in instructional technology from FAU in 2014. Dr. Powers teaches undergraduate and graduate courses in instructional technology and design. Her research focuses on teachers' adoption and integration of technology, preparing pre-service teachers to integrate technology, and STEM education. In 2019, she was selected to be an FAU Woman Leader in STEM.

Email   jrpowers@fau.edu

Why does a business professional need to know this?

Behaviorists believe that all behaviors are learned through conditioning, (interaction with the environment) and can be described and explained without needing to reference mental events or internal psychological processes.

According to this theory, anyone, regardless of their background, can be trained to act in a particular way given the right conditioning. In short, behavior is a response to *environmental stimuli.*

Basic assumptions:

- Behaviorism is primarily concerned with observable behavior, as opposed to internal events like emotions and thinking.
- Behavior is the result of stimulus-response (i.e., all behavior, no matter how complex, is reduced to a stimulus-response relationship).
- Behavior is determined by the environment (e.g., conditioning, nurture).

The birth of behaviorism traces back to the work of John B. Watson in the early 1900s[27]. Watson believed that objective analysis of the mind was impossible. He was a major proponent of shifting the focus of psychology from the mind to behavior. This approach of observing and influencing behavior by focusing on observable, quantifiable events became known as behaviorism.

Behavioral learning theory helps someone who designs learning programs to apply appropriate instructional strategies to achieve results aligned with the needs of the audience and goals of the organization.

Learning is central to the success of every organization. Every business professional can benefit from understanding and applying principles, such as behaviorism, that make the learning process as efficient and effective as possible.

Jennifer Hofmann
Blended Learning

What is it?
A type of learning (also called hybrid learning) that combines appropriate technology with one or more traditional instructional, technical, organizational, or delivery components to present content that supports learners and raises their levels of engagement and achievement.

Why is it important?
Blended learning provides a framework that combines instructional technologies with traditional educational techniques to provide solutions for modern learners working in a business climate that's increasingly mobile, global, and reliant on *collaborative social technologies*.

About Jennifer Hofmann
Jennifer Hofmann is a renowned leader in virtual live learning best practices and services. Her company, InSync Training, was recognized by Inc. 500/500 as one of the highest growth professional learning and development companies five times in the last decade and is known within the training industry for its innovative training solutions. InSync perfected virtual live instruction as a methodology decades before the pandemic and continues to dominate that sector through intensive research, specialized instructional design, innovative instructional techniques, and proven content development practices.

Email	jennifer@insynctraining.com
Website	insynctraining.com/
Twitter	@InSyncJennifer
LinkedIn	linkedin.com/in/jennifer-hofmann-dye/

Why does a business professional need to know this?

Today, most learning is blended learning. Learning initiatives include some combination of live learning and self-directed learning, supported by resources like infographics, videos, and *eLearning*. But modern blended learning is more than sequencing different media and activities that happen to be related by topic.

It is about aligning learning objects with the most appropriate instructional strategies, techniques, and technologies while meeting the needs of the organization and modern learners. When designed and implemented effectively, blended learning is powerful. It creates individual resources that support formal, planned learning events, and supports every informal *moment of learning need*. An added benefit is that resources are no longer shelved or filed after the *learning management system (LMS)* has indicated completion; instead, they become crucial references and tools that learners can use after the instructional program has ended.

Blended learning supports enhanced outreach to learners while connecting workforces that are globally dispersed, working virtually, and always on the go. Blended learning resources are accessible to learners at the time and place of their convenience, as well as accommodating individuals with sight, hearing, and mobility impairments. Thus, blended learning makes your talent development initiatives more inclusive.

Blended learning also enables more *authentic learning*, by allowing individuals to learn, recall, and apply what they've learned when and where they need the content and perform their work. Blended *learning campaigns* provide the ability to create *personal learning paths*, allowing individuals to assess their own needs and make informed decisions about how and what to learn.

Excerpted from *Blended Learning*[29].

Vincent Han
Coaching

What is it?

The practice of a trusted individual providing guidance and oversight to support the development of another individual.

Why is it important?

Virtually every successful professional, in any field, has benefited from some form of coaching. It's essential for any organization interested in the development of its people and leaders to understand the role of effective coaching.

About Vincent Han

Vince Han is the founder and CEO of Mobile Coach and a frequent speaker at conferences such as Training Conference, DevLearn, FocusOn, Online Learning, ATDTK and others. He holds an MBA from the MIT Sloan School of Management. Vince is an industry thought-leader for learning and learning technology with an emphasis on artificial intelligence and chatbot technology. Vince has founded several successful technology companies and resides in Utah.

Email	vince@mobilecoach.com
Website	mobilecoach.com
Twitter	@vincehan
LinkedIn	linkedin.com/in/vincehan/

Why does a business professional need to know this?

Coaches are most commonly associated with sports, providing athletes and teams direction toward the goal of winning a game. Some professional athletes employ multiple coaches, each of whom brings a specific expertise such as skill development, diet and nutrition, strength and conditioning, or sports psychology.

The principle of coaching is tried and true and can fully apply in the workplace to help professionals better perform their responsibilities as well as grow in capacity to expand the impact they make on the business.

To be an effective coach, you need to recognize that people need objective feedback, mentorship, and accountability. It is difficult for humans to see outside themselves to have a clear assessment of their strengths and weaknesses. We all have blind spots that impair our personal development and progress.

An effective coach develops a rapport with an individual to provide a framework of development, choosing specific skills or attributes to improve on within a specific timeframe. Coaching in the workplace can be formal or informal, and the coach can be a professionally trained coach, a skilled and caring manager, or a trusted colleague.

Often, organizations will develop a centralized coaching framework to ensure consistent coaching methods throughout their workforce. Many times, this includes training on how to be an effective coach.

In short, if business professionals are genuinely vested in the success of their people, they will do well to have coaching be a vital part of their *learning and development infrastructure* and culture[42].

Phylise Banner
Cognitive Load

What is it?

The mental effort or workload imposed on a person's *working memory* when processing information.

Why is it important?

Understanding cognitive load is crucial for promoting effective learning, decision making, information processing, user experience, productivity, and training outcomes. In the context of learning and development, cognitive load theory provides insights you can apply to instructional design and delivery to improve the learning process.

About Phylise Banner

Phylise Banner is a learning experience designer with more than 25 years of vision, action, and leadership experience in transformational learning and development approaches. A pioneer in online learning, she is an Adobe Education Leader, Certified Learning Environment Architect (CLEA), Project Management Professional (PMP), STC Fellow, performance storyteller, avid angler, and aviation enthusiast. She is also the proud owner of a 1967 Amphicar.

Email	pbanner@gmail.com
Website	phylisebanner.com
Twitter	@phylisebanner
LinkedIn	linkedin.com/in/phylisebanner

Why does a business professional need to know this?

Business professionals who understand cognitive load are likely to better understand the work of their team members, especially those who design marketing and communication materials, learning content, instructional products, product design, and more.

There are three types of cognitive load you should know:

- **Intrinsic:** The inherent complexity of the learning materials or task itself. Some topics or concepts naturally require more mental effort to understand and process. For example, advanced math equations or intricate scientific theories have a higher intrinsic cognitive load.
- **Extraneous:** Mental effort that is not directly relevant to learning or task. Poorly designed materials, irrelevant information, or complicated instructions can increase extraneous cognitive load.
- **Germane:** The mental effort required to engage in meaningful activities, make connections, and integrate new knowledge with existing knowledge. This effort enables us to develop a deeper understanding and foster long-term learning.

An understanding of cognitive load, especially understanding how to reduce extraneous cognitive load, can help you create more efficient and effective work processes, ultimately contributing to better outcomes for your organization.

And it can help you and your team design more user-friendly products, optimize training programs, improve decision-making, and facilitate collaboration, both within your team and across the organization.

Ashley Reardon
Cognitivism

What is it?

A learning theory that conceptualizes learning processes in terms of how the mind receives, organizes, codes, transforms, stores, rehearses, and retrieves information. Learning occurs when information is stored in memory in a meaningful and retrievable manner.

Why is it important?

Cognitive processing starts with the *working memory*, which has a limited capacity and duration in which it can hold information. Through various methods, you can move information from working to *long-term memory*. Once there, you can hold that information for longer periods of time. But you can only access that information if it has been stored in a way that is easy to retrieve.

About Ashley Reardon

Ashley Reardon is the Head of Design & Development for Culture Programs, Legal & Compliance at Meta, where she has been since 2020. For nearly 25 years, her passion has been in using technology to create better, individual-led, learning-by-doing experiences, and over the years, Ashley has been fortunate to develop experience and expertise in everything from eLearning to instructor-led training to performance support to blended solutions. Ashley has a BS in cognitive science from the University of California, Los Angeles, and an MA in learning sciences from Northwestern University.

Email   alafrenais@gmail.com
Website   kineo.com/
LinkedIn linkedin.com/in/ashleyreardon

Why does a business professional need to know this?

Knowing the science can help a business professional structure a better *learning experience*. How information is presented, the context in which it's presented, and even the emotions of the individual at the time can all affect learning.

Far too often there is a tendency to dump information on learners in an unstructured way. This can lead to *cognitive overload*, meaning the brain has no way of focusing on what's important. If you want your communication to have an impact, take these cues from cognitivism:

- Keep topics short and focused, delivering only the most relevant information.
- Set direction for the learners by helping them know what they can expect to get from your training. This acts as an advanced organizer for sorting the new information as they take it in.
- Deliver information in a relevant context, such as a particular job setting. This helps learners tap into what they already know and add to that.

Making intentional decisions about the context, structure, and order may take extra time but doing so ensures a greater level of understanding and deeper levels of retention.

Rhoda Deon
Communities of Practice

What is it?

A group of people pursuing mutual interests or endeavors who deepen their knowledge and skills through regular and ongoing interactions.

Why is it important?

Whether formally sanctioned or self-organizing, Communities of Practice (CoPs) provide an opportunity for individuals to share insights and innovate. Long before Jean Lave and Etienne Wenger[50] introduced CoPs and a series of best practices, these types of groups were an organically forming, ever-evolving phenomenon that supported *knowledge management*. Today, CoPs are hailed as a key strategy to support an organization's competitive edge in a knowledge-based global economy.

About Rhoda Deon

Rhoda Deon, PhD, is a healer, musician and educator. On a mission to normalize the struggle of being human, her frameworks weave mindfulness practices and data analysis techniques together with games of chance. She has served diverse, global learners in K-12, post-secondary, corporate, and non-traditional settings. Rhoda is a co-designer of Conscious Conversations, a card game that uses levity to help people talk openly about their organization's culture and business practices.

Email	rhoda.deon@gmail.com
Website	rhodadeon.com
LinkedIn	linkedin.com/in/rhodadeon

Why does a business professional need to know this?

Communities of Practice (CoPs) are more than a knowledge management strategy in service of a larger business strategy. They are fluid, living repositories of tacit and explicit *domain-specific knowledge*. Knowledge can live within, without, or across personal and professional silos. CoPs codify shared knowledge and shape the identities of their members. Understanding what a CoP is and what it is not is critical to designing as well as nurturing this type of resource.

At the core of this term are two words: *community* and *practice*.

- A *community* does more than bring diverse individuals together based on a set of collective attributes. A community meets the fundamental biological need to feel a sense of belonging.
- A *practice*, on the other hand, can be a way of being or doing, a repeated effort to increase proficiency, or a convention that is routinely followed by others. The very nature of practice simultaneously embodies who we are, what we do, and how we do it.

Creating a CoP and assigning it a digital space is only the first step. How knowledge will be shared is equally important. Opportunities for storytelling, coaching, and apprenticeship must also be present.

Knowing about CoPs empowers a business professional to unite participants around a process of continuous improvement while reminding them that they are not alone.

Dan McCann
Competency-Based Learning

What is it?

The process of learning a skill by performing that skill with consistent repetition and feedback. Also referred to as *competency-based education*.

Why is it important?

People learn by doing. Learning and development specialists often apply the *70-20-10 model*, which says that 70% of what people learn is from job-related experience, 20% from interactions with others, and 10% from formal training or education[54]. This suggests that well over half of learning should be based on the learner performing a skill rather than an instructor or peer presenting knowledge about the skill.

About Dan McCann

Dan McCann is an experienced and dynamic leader with a passion for lifetime learning, growth strategy, and innovation. Dan started his career in sales, co-founded FRONTLINE Selling where he successfully managed the business from start-up through 15 consecutive years of profitable growth. In 2018, Dan launched SymTrain, which is transforming the future of work by automating the process of situational learning. SymTrain customers train and assess sales, service, and support employees faster and better than they ever could using manual alternatives.

Email	dan.mccann@symtrain.com
Website	symtrain.com
Twitter	@symtrain
LinkedIn	linkedin.com/company/symtrain/
Facebook	facebook.com/symtrain/

Why does a business professional need to know this?

To keep pace with innovation and execute on transformative initiatives, organizations need to make skill development, and any needed re-skilling, a core component of the employee journey. And employees need to continue to master new skills as quickly as possible.

Competency-based learning is a key strategy to help companies meet these challenges. It helps ensure that training is relevant to the work by putting the tasks learners will do on the job into the learning content.

Competency-based learning begins with a needs analysis, which identifies the actual competencies required for mastery on the job. Equipped with information from the needs analysis, subject matter experts, and prospective learners, the learning and development team crafts learning content that challenges learners to perform aspects of the work as part of the *curriculum*.

Typically, competency-based learning allows individual learners to practice until they reach a designated mastery level before moving forward. Practice or repetition might take the form of simulation practice, scenarios, timed drills, etc. It might also include peer mentoring, coaching, and demonstration of mastery. This repetition and practice is especially helpful when the job tasks carry a risk of harm or injury.

Successful and effective competency-based learning provides learning content that is as close to real-world experiences as possible. This includes methods such as simulations, scenarios, hand-on exercises, timed drills, task observation with feedback, etc. Well-designed competency-based learning helps learners connect what they are learning to what they will be doing on the job.

Karen Swan
Constructivism

What is it?

The name given to theories of learning grounded in the notion that meaning is imposed on the world rather than extant in it. Constructivists hold that meaning is constructed in our minds as we interact with the physical, social, and mental worlds we inhabit and that we make sense of our experiences by building and adjusting the internal *mental structures* that collect and organize our perceptions of, and reflections on, reality.

Why is it important?

Constructivism is important because it points to the types of activities that support robust learning, namely activities that are learner-centered, social, and active and which incorporate authentic contexts.

About Karen Swan

Karen Swan, who passed away in September 2021, was the Stukel Professor of Educational Research at the University of Illinois Springfield. For more than 20 years, she was a leading teacher and researcher in the field of online learning. She received the Online Learning Consortium (OLC) Outstanding Individual Achievement award, the National University Technology Network (NUTN) Distinguished Service Award, and the Burks Oakley Distinguished Online Teaching Award for her work in this area. In 2010 she was named an OLC Fellow and is a member of the International Adult and Continuing Education Hall of Fame.

Why does a business professional need to know this?

A business professional should know what constructivism means because it is the learning theory most commonly accepted by educators worldwide. It not only describes how we believe people learn, it suggests *pedagogical* strategies to support learning.

Although there are a variety of constructivist theories—cognitive constructivism, constructionism, social constructivism, *situated learning*, distributed cognition—such theories basically represent different points of view on shared assumptions about the nature of learning and the construction of knowledge.

Constructivism refers to a set of psychological theories that share common assumptions about learning and which collectively represent the most widely accepted beliefs about how people learn. According to constructivists, all learning involves *mental construction*, no matter how one is taught.

All learning occurs in our minds as we create and adjust internal mental structures to accommodate our ever-growing and ever-changing stores of knowledge. All knowledge is thus unique to the individual, and all learning is an active process, intimately tied to experience and the contexts of experience, no matter how or where that learning takes place.

Although constructivism is neither a pedagogical theory nor a theory of instruction, it does have implications for both. In particular, it suggests that education should focus on learners and learning and not on teachers and teaching.

Lorraine Weaver
Experiential Learning

What is it?

Gaining knowledge by actively doing something, reflecting upon the experience, allowing these reflections to change your thinking in some way, and then applying this new understanding.

Why is it important?

Experiential learning goes beyond involving students with real-world projects. It uses a cycle of doing something, taking time to observe and reflect, considering how to adjust, trying a new approach, and then reflecting again[84]. It is excellent for mentoring, service learning, project-based learning, action learning, adventure education, case studies, simulation, and gaming, and it has been shown to have a positive impact on learning[82][84].

About Lorraine Weaver

Lorraine Weaver is currently working as an instructional designer at Thompson Rivers University (TRU). Prior to TRU, she completed 20 years of work in the Canadian Forces as an Aerospace Engineering Officer. Her work included engineering, personnel management, mentoring, and training and development. She has completed degrees in BSc (math), MSc (human factors), a graduate diploma in technology-enhanced learning and design, and an MEd.

Email   lweaver2008@gmail.com
LinkedIn   linkedin.com/in/lorraine-weaver-812745150

Why does a business professional need to know this?

As a business professional, you may have the opportunity to engage with employees who have experience with experiential learning, giving your business the benefit their knowledge of new theories and practices in this area. You can look forward to these employees bringing fresh ideas and perspectives into your team as well as providing the opportunity for junior staff to develop mentorship skills[83].

It may also be helpful to understand that potential new employees who have completed experiential learning have some practical experience, but more than that they have been encouraged to deeply reflect on and learn from this experience. This structured reflection can be very valuable[82].

If you are involved in experiential learning projects, it is important for you to understand enough about the term to position yourself for success. It is critical for experiential learning to be set up in a methodical way that aligns your business goals with student learning objectives and course assessments. Otherwise, you may not see the benefits you were hoping for[83]. Additionally, it is important for you to understand the role you will play in the experiential learning process[83][84].

Marek Hyla
Game-based Learning (GBL)

What is it?

Using traits of games (e.g., rules, goals, effort, rewards, competition, etc.) to immerse learners in engaging and risk-free settings that allow and encourage learning by experimentation. Game-based learning presents learning content in a game format, in contrast with *gamification*, which applies gaming principles to more traditional learning methods.

Why is it important?

Game-based learning processes are dynamic and personalized. Properly implemented, game-based learning that uses emotions, cooperation, or competition has the potential to engage busy and easily distracted learners.

About Marek Hyla

Since 1999, Marek has worked with over 100 companies in learning strategies, learning environment development, and instructional design. As a thought leader he manages the network of people involved in innovative initiatives at Accenture. He is the author/co-author of four books (3 in Polish, 1 in English) on the topics of learning technologies, instructional strategies, and design. He is also the creator of learning and development (L&D) industry solutions: supermemo.net, Learning Battle Cards, and Moments that Matter in Learning.

Email	marek.hyla@accenture.com
Website	learningbattlecards.net/
Twitter	@marek_hyla
LinkedIn	linkedin.com/in/marekhyla/

Why does a business professional need to know this?

The steady growth of the game industry demonstrates that the level of engagement triggered by games is in high demand worldwide. Well-designed games immerse people in an experience where time passes by without notice. In this state, learners are engaged, which improves the efficacy of learning.

Gamification applies gaming principles to traditional learning methods to engage and motivate the learners to learn and retain the learning.

Game-based learning presents learning content in a game format. Learners engage with the learning content while playing a game.

The deep concentration and motivation that game-based learning can provide following benefits:

- Supports *progressive learning*
- Helps personalize the learning experience
- Helps learners evaluate from various perspectives (sometimes even in an unconscious way)
- May increase memory capacity by helping trainees remember more and in a deeper way
- May help improve more complex skills, like decision making, strategic thinking, etc.
- Promotes teamwork and collaboration
- Helps improve the ability to cope in a highly competing and demanding environment
- May help improve hand-eye coordination
- May reduce stress levels by creating a safe environment for learning about failure

The organization also benefits in the following ways:

- **Cost optimization**: digital games can be used anywhere, anytime—just for fun, too
- **Employer branding**: the fun factor positively influences perception
- **Effectiveness**: games can make it easier to tie learning goals to the business environment and the company's organizational goals
- **Efficiency**: optimization of costs through personalized delivery

Patrice Torcivia Prusko
Interaction

What is it?

Connecting in an engaging way by truly listening, having empathy, and understanding the perspective of others such that the learners' ways of knowing have deepened or changed in a meaningful way.

Why is it important?

Meaningful interaction is needed to effectively manage conflict, collaborate, influence, and create a sense of belonging and community.

About Patrice Torcivia Prusko

Patrice Torcivia Prusko is Director of Learning Design, Technology and Media within the Harvard Graduate School of Education. She leads the design, development and project management of online and technology-enhanced courses, including the school's first fully online degree program. Patrice holds a BS degree in mechanical engineering, an MBA from Union College, and a PhD in curriculum and instruction from the University at Albany - State University of New York. She researches and presents on compassion fatigue, supporting women in STEM, equitable and inclusive design practices, and global education.

Email   patrice.torcivia@gmail.com
Website   edtechisgorges.com/
Twitter   @profpatrice
LinkedIn   linkedin.com/in/patrice-torcivia-prusko/

Why does a business professional need to know this?

Interaction is a critical attribute for anyone in business. If you are only hearing, rather than listening, you can miss important information, leading to situations such as: developing a solution for the wrong problem, losing talented individuals, or being unable to lead change or move a project successfully forward.

Good interactions also enable you to build human relationships of trust, which you need to effectively give and receive feedback, mentor and coach, and sustain and build business relationships.

In the learning context, some forms of learning content rely on the use of interaction to enhance the experience of learning. Good interaction can also trigger a brain response that aids learners in their ability to absorb and retain content.

The meaning of the term *interaction* changes depending on the type of learning content experienced. For example, in an in-person class, it might be defined as exchanges between learners, such as group work, role playing, or simulation practice. In a self-paced learning context, it is defined by the way the learner uses or experiences the interface, including interactions such as completing the content in the order that they choose, responding to items or questions, or providing feedback upon completion.

Catherine Lombardozzi
Learning Ecosystem

What is it?
The entirety of all the systems, resources, procedures, practices, and people that influence learning for an individual or group, including the interrelationships among these elements.

Why is it important?
In this age of self-directed learning and rapid change, the health of the learning ecosystem is critical. People learn more effectively and contribute more valuably if they can quickly access robust and relevant learning support.

About Catherine Lombardozzi
Catherine Lombardozzi is a lifelong learning and development practitioner and founder of Learning 4 Learning Professionals. Her work focuses on supporting the professional development of designers, facilitators, faculty, consultants, and learning leaders. She is the author of *Learning Environments by Design*.

Email	clombardozzi@l4lp.com
Website	l4lp.com/
Twitter	@L4LP
LinkedIn	linkedin.com/in/catherinelombardozzi/

Why does a business professional need to know this?

Leaders can exert considerable influence on the elements and qualities of a learning ecosystem in an organization, thereby affecting how efficiently and successfully people can develop their knowledge and skills.

A leader's role is to selectively curate the components of the ecosystem, align them toward articulated goals, and troubleshoot any issues that arise. In shaping a learning ecosystem, leaders are very much like gardeners. They select what to plant, ensure adequate water and sunlight, boost nutrients, and prune here and there.

Leaders advocate for elements that enable learning and performance—from training and development programs to searchable databases to enterprise social networks and more. They ensure that people have access to the most useful and relevant resources and facilitate sharing of resources to help spread new knowledge and effective practices. They craft procedures and practices with an eye toward efficiency, productivity, and flexibility for change, and they align them to a common purpose. And leaders bring people together to learn from and with one another.

By managing all of these elements as part of an ecosystem instead of as unrelated pieces, leaders can create reinforcing loops that propel learning and development, positively affecting performance. Just as a biological ecosystem benefits from human intervention to nurture balance and counter destructive forces, the learning ecosystem benefits from a leader's careful cultivation to support people's growth.

Jennifer Mathes
Online Learning

What is it?

An educational delivery model, primarily through an internet-based platform, in which the learning experience is intentionally designed and incorporates best practices to share knowledge (content, learning activities, etc.) while providing thoughtful and well-structured opportunities for engagement.

Why is it important?

We are a global society and many businesses have operations in more than one country. This means that it is not always possible to bring people together for in-person training. Online learning provides the flexibility to provide needed training in a timely and quality manner. This term is important not only to educators but also to parents, business leaders, politicians, and students.

About Jennifer Mathes

Jennifer Mathes, PhD, is CEO at the Online Learning Consortium. She has over 20 years of experience in both public and private higher education where she has supported online learning initiatives since she taught her first online course. She holds a PhD in education from the University of Illinois at Urbana-Champaign where she wrote her dissertation on "Predictors for Student Success in Online Education."

Email   jennifer.mathes@onlinelearning-c.org
Twitter   @DrMathes
LinkedIn   linkedin.com/in/dr-jennifer-mathes-38a2b6a/

Why does a business professional need to know this?

While various forms of distance education have been around forever, online learning is a relatively new modality that has seen significant growth over the past several years. This is true not only because of the flexibility and accessibility it can provide but also because it can be employed anytime and anywhere—even during a natural disaster or other crisis. Business professionals can use online learning to reach employees who are unable to travel to in-person training.

Learners with an internet connection can select learning content that is live at a designated time at a specific internet address (*synchronous* online learning). Or they can select learning content that can be accessed on demand at any time (*asynchronous* online learning).

ELearning is a form of asynchronous, on-demand learning. It may be completed online, but you can also deliver eLearning from a *Learning Management System (LMS)* server that doesn't require access to the internet.

Online learning is finding its place at all educational levels around the world, including K-12, higher education, university, corporate, and government. Education and training will continue to evolve, and online learning is just one part of that evolution. Understanding its current structure can help you determine the future direction of learning in your organization.

Mark McBride
Open Educational Resources (OER)

What is it?

Digital teaching and learning materials that anyone can freely use for nearly any purpose. They are used as an alternative to college textbooks, which are often too expensive.

Why is it important?

Open educational resources (OER) provide a solution to expensive course materials, especially textbooks, which students often have trouble affording. They are typically licensed under a copyright license developed by Creative Commons that allows creators of OER to legally share their work with fellow practitioners. OER holds benefits for instructors who normally teach with traditional course materials. Instructors who use OER typically follow new processes in course preparation that can lead to innovations in teaching.

About Mark McBride

Mark McBride, PhD, is currently the associate director for Libraries, Scholarly Communications, and Museums at Ithaka S+R. He is a thought leader in higher education, with a track record of implementing changes within complex organizations. Mark has worked in public higher education for nearly 20 years, focusing on academic libraries and student access to education. He is a learning scientist, focused on investigation implications of open education in the higher education curriculum.

Email	mark.mcbride@ithaka.org
Twitter	@mcbrarian
LinkedIn	linkedin.com/in/markmcbride/

Why does a business professional need to know this?

The cost savings realized through open educational resources (OER) are easily understood, but the other benefits of OER are just beginning to have a transformative effect on instruction. Benefits include the following:

- Learners can access the content anywhere and anytime.
- OER supplements traditionally used textbooks and lectures
- Teachers can augment existing content with multimedia content or other formats that enhance the experience of learning
- It is easy and fast to update the curriculum

OER holds tremendous promise for businesses as well, as they begin to explore opportunities to upskill and reskill their employees through low- or no-cost educational resources and tools. The benefits listed above apply as much to business as they do to education. As organizations look for ways to improve educational offerings and develop new ones, OER can make it possible to offer broader, and more economical, choices for their employees.

Like the *Massively Open Online Course (MOOC)* phenomena, OER gives businesses opportunities to provide small, discrete upskilling opportunities or large-scale reskilling pathways at a fraction of the cost of traditional training. Additionally, the licensing flexibility of OER allows organizations to legally edit OER content or combine it with in-house content. (See also *open access*)

Ann Musgrove
Problem-Based Learning (PBL)

What is it?

A team, or individual, approach to that encourages exploration along the path to a solution using real-world, complex problems.

Why is it important?

Memorizing the facts and definitions surrounding the knowledge base of a subject is useless if that information cannot be applied in real-world situations. A problem-based learning approach brings real-world problems into the learning process.

About Ann Musgrove

Ann Musgrove, EdD, is an assistant professor of instructional technology at Florida Atlantic University. Her research interests include best practices in online and face-to-face technology integration, always applied with the philosophy of pedagogy before technology. Some of her ongoing interests include the exploratory installations of technology test kitchens, tools to teach information literacy to fight the propagation of fake news, and exploring 1:1 computing in K-12 classrooms.

Email	musgrove.ann@gmail.com
Website	annmusgrove.com
Twitter	@annmusgrove
LinkedIn	linkedin.com/in/ann-musgrove-ed-d-a4b32916/

Why does a business professional need to know this?

Problem-based learning (PBL) takes place in business situations on a daily basis. A group is presented with or discovers a real-world problem that needs to be addressed. Beginning with the end goal in mind the group decides on outcomes and assessments that will show at the end of the process that the problem has been solved. If a scenario isn't already apparent, creating a real-world scenario of the problem aids in the process by framing the research and information gathering process.

The history of PBL includes education in medical schools where it was sometimes evident that students were well equipped with medical knowledge but lacking in their ability to apply that knowledge in the real world. This gap between knowledge and practice was filled with common and challenging medical problems solved by a group of medical students using discussion and research to come up with a plan to help the patient.

K-12 schools have also embraced PBL for many of the same reasons medical education did. PBL encourages active learning and creativity and places more responsibility on the students with the teacher guiding the learning path.

Jennifer Staley
Scaffolding

What is it?

A method of instructor-led teaching that begins with the instructor providing a lot of support (scaffolding) to the learner, then reducing that support as the learner gains proficiency, allowing the learner to become more and more independent.

Why is it important?

Scaffolding is important because it allows learners to build from their current knowledge and experiences through temporary, but supportive, learning interactions, which act as building blocks towards the acquisition of new knowledge and skills.

About Jennifer Staley

Jennifer Staley is SVP of Operations of Shoulder2Shoulder, Inc. a Certified Service Disabled Veteran Owned Small Business. Jennifer has been a talent and organizational development professional for over two decades across multiple industries and has an enthusiasm for continued education and lifelong learning experiences. Jennifer continues to shape her instructional design principles and strategies, her philosophy and vision for learning and performance in both her professional and personal lives.

Email	staley.jen@gmail.com
Twitter	@jennystaley
LinkedIn	linkedin.com/in/jennystaley
Facebook	facebook.com/jennystaley

Why does a business professional need to know this?

Business professionals who implement scaffolding in learning and development initiatives—whether at the group, department, or enterprise level—provide a critical, temporary support that not only enables their workforce to be supported and elevated in their learning acquisition but also provides a metric against which they can measure the effectiveness of those initiatives.

Consider the following:

- Could a construction and facilities engineer build a multi-story building without building scaffolding to support the construction?
- Could a project manager manage a multi-year, multi-million-dollar contract, including the schedule and costs, without a work breakdown structure and a framework to support project planning and scheduling?

Not using scaffolding in these contexts can be compared to a learning-and-development professional not integrating scaffolding into learning activities. Without scaffolding, there would be no supports to guide the learner through the learning process.

Most of us need some type of support when learning something new or shoring up our current understanding. When we have learned what is needed, we move up to the next level and don't need to rely on that support any longer.

Building scaffolding supports into learning and development creates a positive and empowering learning environment.

Jane Bozarth
Social and Informal Learning

What is it?
Acquiring new information and skills by watching and interacting with others, or on one's own, apart from or in addition to, traditional formal instruction.

Why is it important?
Social learning is participative and might occur in either/both formal and informal environments. However, informal learning is mostly unplanned and impromptu in nature. Social learning is important because much of workplace learning happens in social and informal ways.

About Jane Bozarth
Jane Bozarth, EdD, holds a master's degree in technology in training and a doctorate in training and development. Over the past two decades, she has worked as a classroom designer, trainer, eLearning specialist, social media specialist, and organization research director.

Dr. Bozarth is the author of many books, including *eLearning Solutions on a Shoestring* and *From Analysis to Evaluation*. She is a popular conference speaker and appears at many industry events.

Email	info@bozarthzone.com
Website	bozarthzone.com
Twitter	@JaneBozarth
LinkedIn	linkedin.com/in/janebozarth
Facebook	facebook.com/Bozarthzone

Why does a business professional need to know this?

While the terms *social learning* and *informal learning* (also called *tacit knowledge*) have seen increased use over the past decade or so, the ideas aren't new at all. Most of what we know we learned socially. Think about how you learned to speak your native language or how you acquired the skills necessary to abide by unwritten rules and norms in a new workplace. While other means of learning, such as *operant conditioning*, do play a role—we learn not to touch a hot stove after doing it once—a great deal of what we know comes from moving in the world, engaging with and watching others.

Likewise, much of what we know is learned informally and serendipitously: our parents typically didn't sit us down and run through flashcards of verb conjugations. Rather, we learned in the moment, as conversations evolved and new situations arose.

These terms are primarily used in education to distinguish them from traditional, formal instruction delivered as structured, one-way teacher-to-student interactions. While many believe that learning must always look like school, it's important to recognize how pervasive and valid other means of learning are.

Those responsible for employee development efforts as managers, or in workforce development as learning practitioners, can shore up learning by offering ample opportunities for social interaction—both in person and via electronic means—and the time and resources for self-directed acquisition of new information and skills.

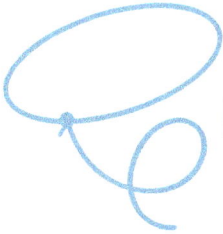

Implementation

Implementation implies putting plans into action. In the learning space this involves the consideration of tools, technologies, methodologies, and procedures that would best support the realization of our learning designs.

The terms in this book that fall under the category of implementation define the approaches we take to transforming learning designs into tangible, measurable learning experiences.

Terms in this section:

- Curation
- Curriculum
- Delivery Mode
- Knowledge Transfer
- Learning Content Standards
- Learning Management System
- Learning Objectives

David Kelly
Curation

What is it?
Selecting, vetting, organizing, and distributing effective content.

Why is it important?
The amount of information available to workers is increasing at an exponential rate. Business professionals have neither the time nor the expertise needed to identify the most valuable content from this seemingly endless flow. Curation selects and presents the most useful, valuable content and makes it available so others don't need to repeat that effort. In his book *Curation Nation*[62], Steven Rosenbaum describes it this way: "Curation replaces noise with clarity."

About David Kelly
David Kelly is the CEO of The Learning Guild. Before joining the Guild, David has been a learning and performance consultant and training director for over 20 years. He is a leading voice exploring how technology can be used to enhance training, education, learning, and organizational performance.

Email	dkelly@elearningguild.com
Website	learningguild.com
Twitter	@LnDDave
LinkedIn	linkedin.com/in/lnddave/

Why does a business professional need to know this?

Business professionals should care because curation is emerging as an important competency. In today's world of work the person who knows everything is no longer the most valuable member of the team; the person who can find and share the answer to anything is.

Museum curators don't create content. They listen, then find content that resonates. They scour the globe for artifacts related to that content and organize artifacts in such a way that guests are taken on a learning journey as they experience an exhibit. Of course, museum curators are highly trained for doing this. It is their specialty.

Business professionals are finding that curation is an important specialty in their world, too. Curation in the business world starts from the assumption that most questions have already been answered and most problems have already been solved. Curation finds the answers to those questions and the solutions to those problems and makes the results available. Good curation can help your organization and its customers become more efficient both in learning and in everyday operations.

How does curation fit into learning and performance? The most visible form of curation comes from informal learning that takes place on the job through coaching, mentoring, experiences, and sharing. But capturing this type of learning is difficult, because it takes place serendipitously and without documentation. Actively seeking to capture that knowledge and pass it on is valuable both to the company and its employees.

Business professionals can also curate the information they provide to customers to ensure that they do not overwhelm customers with irrelevant information. Curation, as a discipline, can help replace noise with clarity and enable you to deliver solutions faster and more efficiently.

Bryan Alexander
Curriculum

What is it?

Any sequence of planned activities or experiences that enables learners to explore materials, practice what they have learned, and achieve proficiency.

Why is it important?

Central to all learning experiences, a curriculum provides the core structure that guides learners on their path to meet set goals. In other words, a curriculum helps learners learn by creating a framework that communicates performance standards, key learnings, methods, projects, relevant metrics, evaluation plans, etc.

About Bryan Alexander

Bryan Alexander is an education and technology futurist. A senior scholar at Georgetown University, he helps colleges, universities, libraries, non-profits, and governments think about where education may be going in the coming decades. Creator of the Future of Education Observatory, Bryan publishes the monthly FTTE trends report, conducts the weekly Future Trends Forum, blogs, and runs an online book club. He speaks, consults, and publishes widely. His latest book is *Universities on Fire: Higher Education in the Climate Crisis* (Johns Hopkins University Press).

Email	bryan.alexander@gmail.com
Website	futureofeducation.us/
Twitter	@bryanalexander
LinkedIn	linkedin.com/in/bryannalexander
Facebook	facebook.com/bryannalexander

Why does a business professional need to know this?

Imagine trying to assemble a structure without a cohesive plan. Yes, it is possible to build something, but how will you measure progress along the way? And how will you be able to recreate what was built later?

Creating a curriculum is creating a plan that lays out a set of expectations to help learners build towards their goals. The curriculum might include a sequence of courses, internships, mentorships, coaching sessions, or immersive simulations that, in essence, serve as the building blocks of learning.

Establishing a curriculum, in alignment with business or educational goals, provides a roadmap that enables learners to progress along learning pathways in support of their own or organizational growth. Alignment also enables learning leaders to invest in the future of their people in the organization and report to stakeholders on how their educational programs support the mission and vision of the organization.

John Vivolo
Delivery Mode

What is it?

The way learning content is presented to learners. Possibilities include in-person, lecture, digital, electronic, synchronous, asynchronous, and more.

Why is it important?

Delivery mode is important because the right delivery mode can help showcase content more effectively and facilitate learning and retention. While it is often considered a static concept that is either a designated location or type of technology, delivery mode is neither static nor one size fits all. Instead, the delivery mode should be chosen based on what is to be learned *and* the needs of the learners. Delivery mode can also be combination of two or more modes, often referred to as taking a blended approach.

About John Vivolo

For nearly 20 years, John Vivolo has dedicated his career to online learning. His experience includes being an instructor, instructional designer, educational technologist, director of an award-winning online learning unit at New York University (NYU) and, more recently, executive director at the Katz School of Science and Health. John is currently all-but-dissertation in the EdD program at Northeastern University.

Email   johnvivolo@yahoo.com
Twitter   @vivolojohn
LinkedIn   linkedin.com/in/johnvivolo/

Why does a business professional need to know this?

Business professionals need to have an understanding of delivery modes so they can work with learning and development professionals to select the best delivery mode(s) for their needs. Factors to consider when selecting a delivery mode include:

- Business reasons for requiring learners to complete training
- Who the learners are, e.g., new staff or experienced staff
- The learners' current skill levels
- Available resources, including people, budget, and time
- How soon the learning needs to become a part of the learners' routine
- Size of the learner population
- Aspects of existing training that are no longer relevant or effective
- Nature of the content, e.g., completely new or a refresher
- Complexity of the content
- How learner proficiency will be evaluated, e.g., quizzes, proficiency tests, timed drills, observation, problem solving, and so forth.

Knowing the responses to these considerations can help you or your instructional designer assess how best to present the content. Methods for presenting content include the following:

- Demonstration
- Distance learning, whether synchronous or asynchronous
- eLearning
- Hands-on learning
- Informal learning
- Lecture
- Lab
- Job aids or *performance support* tools, e.g., labeled images, checklists, or step-action tables
- Projects, e.g., individual or group
- Peer mentoring and coaching
- Microlearning modules
- Simulation, whether on the job or using augmented or virtual reality
- Social learning
- Solving problems or resolving challenges
- Video, e.g., tutorial, scenario, simulation, or interactive video

Jamye Sagan
Knowledge Transfer

What is it?

Collecting and curating knowledge from experienced workers and sharing it with others, especially those who will continue their work.

Why is it important?

Experienced workers possess vast knowledge about their jobs and roles. When these workers leave, whether through retirement or other reasons, their work still must continue. Without some form of knowledge transfer, all that collective knowledge walks away with them.

Knowledge transfer helps businesses identify, understand, and document what must be done, so operations continue after an experienced worker leaves.

About Jamye Sagan

Jamye Sagan has over 15 years of technical communication experience. As the pharmacy communication advisor for H-E-B (Texas-based grocery chain), she helps design training programs and deliverables, while managing communications between corporate and retail. Jamye also volunteers with the Society for Technical Communication in various capacities and has spoken about instructional design, all while sharing her love of knitting, Harry Potter, and cats. She lives in San Antonio, TX.

Email	jamye.sagan@gmail.com
Twitter	@gimli_the_kitty
LinkedIn	linkedin.com/in/jamye-sagan-15416434/
Facebook	facebook.com/jamye.sagan

Why does a business professional need to know this?

Knowledge transfer isn't just about writing step-by-step procedures on how to carry out a particular function. It also entails any activity in which experienced workers share their knowledge, including mentoring, videos, and even informal chats.

Although many aspects of knowledge transfer relate to older generations who are beginning to retire from the workplace, the term *experienced worker* pertains to anyone, regardless of age, who has significant experience in a particular realm.

Knowledge transfer is not just sharing the *what* or *how* but also *why* things are done. When businesses can tap into this collective wisdom, they will have not only clear-cut documentation for others to follow but also building materials through which to analyze the big picture, so they can potentially streamline processes or see where to allocate resources more efficiently.

Be aware that some workers may feel threatened by being asked to share what they know. They may fear that their jobs will become obsolete or, worse, that they will be made to feel useless. Although knowledge transfer is vital to continuing operations, it's crucial to remember that we are dealing with people first and foremost. Businesses must remain sensitive to these feelings and reassure experienced workers that they are not simply being siphoned for their knowledge and later discarded.

Overall, knowledge transfer helps businesses not only capture knowledge but also potentially identify more efficient processes. Ultimately, successful knowledge transfer can save money and time because of these efficiencies and the ease with which successors can pick up the torch.

Adam Weisblatt
Learning Content Standards

What is it?

A set of tools, processes, templates, and conventions that ensure that the materials created to support learning in an organization are consistently designed, developed, deployed, and tracked in support of business goals.

Why is it important?

Learning takes resources. To obtain the resources needed to sustain a learning culture, you need to think strategically about how you will use those resources. Having a strategy with respect to learning content standards helps ensure that decisions about allocating resources are always made in the context of the bigger picture.

About Adam Weisblatt

Adam Weisblatt is passionate about building the resilience of learning and development organizations so they can create business value. Adam has experience in all aspects of workplace learning and a proven track record of implementing global enterprise-wide projects using an agile, collaborative, and creative approach to meeting organizational needs. He has the ability to analyze systems, processes, and team dynamics and uses outstanding visuals and storytelling to explain them to a wide audience. He provides consulting and design services for companies throughout their digital transformation. Adam speaks at conferences and writes for industry magazines. He is also a cartoonist and puppeteer.

Email   adamjweisblatt@gmail.com
Twitter   @weisblatt
LinkedIn   linkedin.com/in/adamjweisblatt/

Why does a business professional need to know this?

Business professionals know that learning is a key strategic activity. However, learning departments are under pressure to reduce costs and justify their spending. Because they are a cost center, they must have a demonstrable strategy as to how they deliver value and manage costs. Having solid learning content standards helps ensure that their investment is worthwhile and reflects the needs of the business.

Learning content standards help leverage the power of these technologies:

- **Learning Management System (LMS):** a platform to support the deployment of learning events, launch learning content, and return data about the completion of learning experiences and satisfaction of learning requirements. Note: one reason eLearning is possible is because an LMS can record course completion without the intervention of an instructor (see *Learning Management System*).

- **Learning Experience Platform (LXP):** a platform to enable users to find needed learning experiences by organizing resources based on their relevance to skills, business goals, and related offerings[117].

- **eXperience Application Programming Interface (xAPI):** a standard for capturing and storing data about learner behavior. xAPI can capture test scores and completion status as well as other information about what users do during the learning experience[116].

Phily Hayes
Learning Management System (LMS)

What is it?

A software application used to administer, track, report, and deliver training to a range of learners, including internal employees, software users, and university students.

Why is it important?

Learning management systems (LMS) make it easier to disperse knowledge to multiple audiences and make eLearning more efficient, scalable, and effective. LMS technology is evolving, and with newer technologies, they are becoming more widely used in the corporate environment.

About Phily Hayes

Phily Hayes has worked on 100s of LMS implementations from the vendor side and spoken at multiple conferences internationally on the topic.

Email   phily@zerve.ai

Why does a business professional need to know this?

A large part of how businesses create value is through distributing knowledge. Knowledgeable employees are able to effectively help their customers, knowledgeable customers are able to successfully use the business's products, and knowledgeable prospective customers are able to confidently choose the right product in the first place. A learning management system helps businesses systematically store, deliver, and track content so they can more effectively distribute knowledge.

If your company does not have an LMS, you should investigate to see if one can help your company. If you do much in-house training, the odds are that one will.

If your company has an LMS, then you should gain at least a basic understanding of its capabilities and its impact on your business. This enables you to take advantage of those capabilities to increase your knowledge, and the knowledge of your employees.

Capabilities vary by vendor, what features have been purchased, and what level of access you are allowed to have. If you know the features that are available to you, you can make the best possible use of your LMS.

Julie Dirksen
Learning Objectives

What is it?

A statement of one or more goals of a learning experience that identifies the specific knowledge, skills, or behaviors that a learner should be able to demonstrate after the learning experience.

Why is it important?

Learning objectives are the foundation upon which a curriculum is based, and good clear learning objectives can be critical for creating good instruction. Sometimes, designers differentiate between "learning objectives" and "performance objectives" but learning design for adults should be guided by the concrete, visible behaviors that the learner will actually need to perform in the real world.

About Julie Dirksen

Julie Dirksen is a consultant and instructional designer with more than 20 years' experience creating interactive e-Learning experiences. She loves brains, and games and evidence-based practice, and her current focus is the science of behavior change. She wrote the book *Design For How People Learn*, and she's happiest whenever she gets to learn something new.

Email	julie@usablelearning.com
Website	usablelearning.com
Twitter	@usablelearning
LinkedIn	linkedin.com/in/juliedirksen/
Facebook	facebook.com/groups/designforhowpeoplelearn/

Why does a business professional need to know this?

Developing learning objectives is one place where a business professional can collaborate with learning professionals to ensure that the business goals for the organization align with the educational offerings the organization offers.

Collaboration between business and learning professionals can create learning objectives that will guide the curriculum development process. Good learning objectives help you eliminate unnecessary content that doesn't support your business objectives. Learning objectives also help you focus the learner's attention, evaluate the effectiveness of training, and establish performance standards.

A single set of learning objectives may not serve all those purposes, and you may need to have different versions of learning objectives for different audiences or purposes.

Business professionals can also benefit from learning objectives because they document the goals of a training activity and provide a benchmark for assessing the value of training.

Evaluation

Evaluation methods tell us whether our learners are actually learning—if they are gaining knowledge, skills, techniques, aptitudes, etc. Evaluation can also refer to the approaches we take to test the validity of our work and determine what needs to be fixed or improved.

The terms in this book that fall under the category of evaluation support how, where, when, and why we review that evidence of learning and what we do when our learners fail, succeed, or get lost while traveling along their learning journeys.

Terms in this section:

- Accreditation
- Assessment
- Certification
- Digital Badges
- Engagement
- Evaluation (Formative and Summative)
- Feedback
- Human Performance Improvement

Karan Powell
Accreditation

What is it?

The process whereby a third-party authority acknowledges or affirms that academic, business, or industry quality standards have been met by an organization.

Why is it important?

Accreditation sets an organization apart because it proves that the organization has been assessed against the accrediting body's defined standards in a professional or academic area and been found to meet those standards. Accreditation is important because it may be required in order for a company to operate in certain areas. For example, academic accreditation is required for a college or university to offer degree programs.

About Karan Powell

Karan Powell, PhD, is president of KHP Consulting, providing organization transformation consulting and coaching services to higher education and business. Dr. Powell is president (retired) of American Public University System, having 35+ years in higher education as faculty, administrator, and executive. Dr. Powell was instrumental in earning and maintaining regional and multiple specialty accreditations during her tenure at APUS and has 15+ years of service on the peer review corps of an institutional accreditor.

Email   dr_kmhp@outlook.com

Why does a business professional need to know this?

Accreditation is an indicator of the quality and effectiveness of the services or products an organization provides. Some industries, such as education, healthcare, information technology, travel, engineering, fire and security, and public health, require industry accreditation. Business professionals can use accreditation as part of evaluating potential business partners or vendors.

Regulations for required accreditation in particular industries may vary by country or nation and in some cases by state. Accreditation is specific to a particular institution and indicates that the institution (hospital, college, school, etc.) or a particular program (specialty accreditation) within the institution meets the accrediting body's standards. Accreditation by a third-party accreditor indicates that the provider meets certain standards essential to providing services in that industry or practice.

Related to accreditation, but different from it, are *certification* and *licensure*. Some industries require individuals to be certified (to have completed a recognized program of study, such as some IT certifications) or licensed (to have passed state or national standards to be able to practice in areas such as law and medicine). Certificates are usually earned by individuals. Licensure can apply to an individual or to an institution.

These regulatory requirements aim to ensure that consistent quality standards for care or service are provided to customers of that particular industry or service. Each business needs to understand and comply with the requirements for accreditation for their industry and the requirements for certification and licensure for their employees.

Myra Travin
Assessment

What is it?
An assortment of methods and tools used to measure the acquisition of knowledge and skills one has acquired during a course of study.

Why is it important?
Assessments are one way to determine what someone has learned at a particular point during a course. For example, end-of-course or section testing can assess a learner's progress, which can then be compared with expected outcomes. Results are not always meant to be final, but they can be guideposts to help learners know where they might need help.

About Myra Travin
Myra Travin is an accomplished educational program manager and learning solutions designer, known for implementing innovative programs in global IT, leadership, change management, and performance. As a respected industry leader, Myra speaks at top conferences such as SXSW, SciTS, and ATD, and has been published in Training Magazine and major US newspapers. Her passion for creating impactful learning experiences inspires others to embrace learning innovation and drive meaningful change.

Email   myratravin48@gmail.com
Website   myratravin.me
LinkedIn   linkedin.com/in/myratravin

Why does a business professional need to know this?

As the science of assessment changes, so does the definition of assessment and testing. Technology and the pace of information transfer are both critical factors that have an impact on the science and practice of assessment. Technology advances in *performance support* tools have given you a more granular view into the learning experience. In addition, data and learning analytics reveal factors about the performance of an individual that couldn't be measured before.

Business professionals can take advantage of these advances to better understand how effective their training is. Of course, business professionals need to remember that assessments are only as good as the data from which they were created. The old maxim, garbage in garbage out, applies here.

Because assessments are often linked to *ROI* in corporate settings or funding initiatives in educational ones, they can be highly political. The elephant in the room is that testing or assessment data is often manipulated to show better results than actually exist.

Accepting this reality is a practical place to start any methodology related to assessment. What is essential to assessment is accurate data collection and honest reporting of the data and conclusions. If the data you collect is relevant to the learning outcomes, then the data will be accurate.

At the end of the day, the most important piece of assessment is data accuracy. What good does it do to record data if it is not accurate? You must begin by being very careful about what you measure, why you measure it, and what its relationship is to your learners' performance.

Saul Carliner
Certification

What is it?

A validation of competence, as compared against a set of standards and rigor, by a third-party certifying organization. Certification is like *licensing*, but licenses are legally required for certain jobs. Certifications are voluntary.

Why is it important?

The knowledge, skill, and attitudes assessed for a certification come from a competency model, which is a framework of interrelated knowledge, skills, attitudes, and values derived through a rigorous research and validation process.

Certification plays two roles in the work of professionals. It may be required as a work assignment, or a person may choose to seek certification. Certifications exist in many fields. See the notes for several in the learning field[37][38][39].

About Saul Carliner

Saul Carliner, PhD, CTDP, is a Professor of Educational Technology at Concordia University in Montreal. Also an industry consultant, he specializes in the design of instructional and informational materials for the workplace, managing groups who produce those materials, and related issues of policy and professionalism. His books include the best-selling *Training Design Basics*, award-winning *Informal Learning Basics*, and the recent *An Overview of Training and Development: Why Training Matters and Career Anxiety: Guidance Through Tough Times*. He is President of the Canadian Network for Innovation in Education, a Fellow and past board member of the Institute for Performance and Learning, and a Fellow and past international president of the Society for Technical Communication.

Email   saulcarliner@hotmail.com

Why does a business professional need to know this?

Business professionals might encounter certification in their work. They might also be responsible for launching or managing a certification program and need an awareness of how to create and manage these programs.

Establishing a certification program includes the development of:

- A competency model
- A certification exam
- Assessment criteria for demonstrating competence
- Training to ensure that *assessors* act consistently
- Requirements for maintaining the certification
- A *code of ethics* to which professionals who receive certification must adhere
- Training to prepare people for certification

If you are seeking certification, whether for yourself or members of your staff, make sure that the certification is a useful credential—rather than a certificate that is inappropriately marketed—and that hiring managers recognize the certification.

Business professionals might also need to assess or validate a certification provided on a job applicant's resume to determine whether the certification validates the competence claimed by the applicant.

Certification is often confused with certificates. A certificate recognizes the successful completion of the requirements of an educational program. However, those who receive certificates are not certified. Certification typically requires a test of knowledge, ensuring familiarity with the body of knowledge of the field and its application in common work situations. Candidates must also demonstrate competence at doing the work, as assessed by a review of completed work or a demonstration of skills to a panel of assessors. Certification may also require real work experience, meaning a minimum specified number of years working in the field.

Most certifications require maintenance or re-certification through the completion of continuing education and other requirements to stay current in the field.

Chris Price
Digital Badges

What is it?

A way to demonstrate and communicate an achievement to a wide variety of online platforms.

Why is it important?

Being able to communicate effectively what you know and are able to do to others is an essential component of being an effective learner and successful in your career.

About Chris Price

Chris Price is the academic programs manager for the SUNY Center for Professional Development (CPD). At the CPD, Chris designs and implements professional development programs for faculty and staff both in and outside SUNY. Prior to his position with CPD, Chris was director of the Center for Excellence in Learning and Teaching at The College at Brockport, SUNY, for 12 years. He received his PhD in political science from the University at Albany in 2004.

Email   chris.price@suny.edu
Twitter   @chrisprice117
LinkedIn   linkedin.com/in/chrisprice117

Why does a business professional need to know this?

Successful learners do more than accumulate knowledge and skills. It is also important to communicate effectively what you know and are able to do. On the surface, a digital badge typically consists of a brief title and an image representing an activity. When you click on the badge you access the details of the activity, including who issued the badge, what was done to earn the badge, and sometimes a link to evidence demonstrating the skill or knowledge signified by the badge.

A digital badge is more specific than a resume or CV (which is only a summary of your experience and credentials) or an academic transcript (which typically lists only courses and grades).

Digital badges are commonly issued to recognize achievement in formal educational settings as well as in continuing education, training, and professional development. A digital badge is easily shared via online platforms like LinkedIn, Facebook, or Twitter and can also be embedded in a web page or *e-portfolio*.

As you accumulate badges, you acquire a visual representation and summary of your knowledge and skills, making it easier to identify strengths and gaps in your education and professional development activities.

Digital badges also help *gamify* an experience when grouped together to demonstrate an increasing level of mastery. Digital badges can be *stacked* into something more comprehensive that is sometimes labeled a *micro-credential*.

Kassy LaBorie
Engagement

What is it?

The degree to which a learner pays attention to the content and interactions, reacts to and participates in the activities, and responds to the instructor, other learners, and technology throughout a learning experience.

Why is it important?

Engagement traditionally is one of the first indicators of whether learning has a chance to be effective. Engagement does not need to be connected to liking something or disliking it, though disliking something may lead to disengagement. It's important to understand how engagement is connected to retention and application, how it differs among learners, and how to build it into learning programs in ways that appeal to a variety of learners.

About Kassy LaBorie

Kassy LaBorie is the principal consultant at Kassy LaBorie Consulting. She is a professional speaker, author, and facilitator who specializes in virtual engagement using web conferencing technology to connect around the globe. She's known for believing that being online is certainly equal to, and in some cases, better than, being in-person! She has authored *Interact and Engage! 75+ Activities for Virtual Training, Meetings, and Webinars*, and *Producing Virtual Training, Meetings, and Webinars* with ATD Press.

Email	kassy.laborie@gmail.com
Website	kassyconsulting.com/
Twitter	@KassyConsulting
LinkedIn	linkedin.com/in/kassylaborie/

Why does a business professional need to know this?

Ask a learning and development professional what's most important in a training initiative and their first response is likely to be: engagement. The participants need to be engaged, the trainer needs to know how to engage them, and the topic needs to be put together in a way that is compelling.

Research has repeatedly shown that engagement is directly connected to retention[76][77]. A learner must respond to the training content and then remember it for any training experience to be applied on the job.

Here are 5 simple ways to create engagement and motivate learners:

1. Create friendly, open, safe, and encouraging learning environments where participants feel comfortable taking chances and at ease communicating with the instructor and one another.
2. Set clear expectations for the learning goals and objectives. Participants are engaged when they know what they are doing, why they need to do it, how it will be accomplished, and what, exactly, a successful outcome looks like.
3. Challenge participants to be active with the learning process, to do something with the content being covered, and to find their own ways to apply it in their own environments.
4. Reward and recognize their efforts. Participants engage when they are seen, heard, and included.
5. Stay connected with open communication and dialogue, allowing participants the flexibility to adjust how they are learning, work through challenges with assignments, and build camaraderie with the instructor and others along the way.

Alexander Salas
Evaluation

What is it?
The methodology by which we validate the results of a given *learning strategy*.

Why is it important?
There's no greater challenge for those that have the great responsibility and privilege to support organizational performance than to show the effectiveness of their efforts. More often than not, learning and development (L&D) teams are very efficient at developing solutions but not so much at evaluating them. Evaluation is critical to demonstrating whether your learning efforts are worth their cost.

About Alexander Salas
Alexander Salas is an award-winning instructional designer with over 15 years of experience specializing in the blend of learning technologies and gamification for performance outcomes. Since 2007, Alex has worked in every facet of corporate learning and performance enablement for Fortune 100 enterprises such as Philips Healthcare, Centene Corporation and Dell Technologies. When he's not creating amazing learning experiences, you can find Alex giving back to the industry at large with articles, workshops, conferences, and podcasting.

Email   asalas@stylelearn.com
Website   stylelearn.com
LinkedIn   linkedin.com/in/stylelearn/

Why does a business professional need to know this?

Business professionals need to justify educational programs. In addition to measuring learner performance, evaluations can form an important tool for making a business case for your learning programs.

You can use evaluations in two roles. Formative evaluations (is it working?) take place while content is being designed or delivered. They can take many forms, including surveys and tests. They determine whether things are going well. Summative evaluations are an after-action report on the learning content (did it work?).

In 1959, Donald Kirkpatrick created the four levels of training evaluation, with the aim of guiding the evaluation of educational courses [80]. The four levels are Reaction, Learning, Behavior, and Results. Here is a summary of the levels:

- **Level One, Reaction:** The learner's reaction to the experience. Kirkpatrick called this a measure of customer satisfaction.
- **Level Two, Learning:** Change in attitude, knowledge, or skill.
- **Level Three, Behavior:** Observable changes in learner behavior. For example, people are trained to use a new piece of machinery; supervisor attests to proficiency on the job.
- **Level Four, Results:** Achievement of the initial objectives. For example, did sales increase? Were accidents reduced? Has employee turnover changed for the better?

Evaluation results are only as good as the objectives they refer to. Without a proper analysis of needs, most efforts will suffer from GIGO (Garbage-In, Garbage-Out) problems. Regardless of the model and scope of the evaluation, it is good to use both formative and summative approaches.

Theresa Hummel-Krallinger
Feedback

What is it?
Information, solicited or unsolicited, that provides an opinion on how a person has performed something.

Why is it important?
We are a work in progress. Each of us is at a unique point in our personal and professional journey, and we all have things that we can improve. Feedback is an important source of input to help us improve. Ask: *How am I doing? What might I do better?* Depending on self-awareness level, feedback is an excellent way to start on a journey of self-improvement.

Feedback is a gift. Sometimes it is criticism. It is still valuable information from which to operate. Ask: *Is this a belief I want them to have?* If not, seek ways to change that belief. Don't filter feedback. Ask questions to clarify.

And always say *thank you.*

About Theresa Hummel-Krallinger
Theresa is an award-winning comedian, having won two Emmys for her work on the PBS talk show, "Counter Culture." She is a well-respected training professional and performance consultant. Known for her lively and interactive presentation style, she is a frequently requested speaker on leadership, career management, organizational culture and workplace communications. She has been a featured speaker at numerous regional and international conferences.

Email	tkrallinger@highfiveperformance.com
Website	highfiveperformance.com/
Twitter	@theresahk
LinkedIn	linkedin.com/in/tkrallinger/
Facebook	facebook.com/theresahkcomedy

Why does a business professional need to know this?

Every solid business professional acknowledges the importance of feedback. It should be something that you seek out for personal and professional growth. It is also something that a good business professional is willing to proactively share with others in an effort to help them learn and grow.

Providing good feedback should be a pleasure! As a practice, you might want to mark your calendar every week for some time to send positive feedback and thank you notes. Regularly sharing good feedback and appreciation will build trust and respect with your colleagues and staff.

Providing constructive feedback should be done tactfully and with care. It's important that the recipient of the constructive feedback understand your motive. If someone trusts you and believes you care about their success, they are more likely to receive and use the feedback. If they question your motive, they may not appreciate the feedback, and in some cases, might get defensive. As best you can, make it safe, and ensure they understand your intention. Like all things, practice makes perfect. The more you share feedback, the better you'll get.

The most successful business professionals are adept at both giving and soliciting feedback. It's worth the time and effort!

Marjorie Derven
Human Performance Improvement

What is it?

A methodology for improving the performance of individuals and organizations. Human performance improvement (HPI) looks for performance gaps, analyzes root causes, and helps you create a plan that produces sustainable performance improvements.

Why is it important?

HPI is a systematic process that improves your ability to identify and address the root causes of performance issues. It helps you build effective partnerships and allocate resources to create lasting solutions to performance problems. The HPI process is multidimensional, addressing issues such as learning gaps, organizational culture, leadership issues, rewards and recognition, and other barriers to desired performance.

About Marjorie Derven

Marjorie Derven is a change management consultant with RGP, a global consulting firm that enables rapid business outcomes by bringing together the right people to create transformative change. Marjorie has worked with many of the world's best companies to align people practices with strategic imperatives. She has served on NY HR Strategy & People, ATD, and the OD Practitioner boards and as a senior fellow at The Conference Board. Marjorie is a frequent presenter at global conferences and has authored dozens of articles.

Email	marjoriederven@gmail.com
Website	rgp.com
Twitter	@mderven
LinkedIn	linkedin.com/in/marjoriederven/

Why does a business professional need to know this?

In today's highly interconnected, fast-changing organizational environment, addressing pressing challenges and opportunities requires a multifaceted approach. Enter human performance improvement, a process that enables you to better understand root causes and deploy a systems approach to create end-to-end solutions that produce sustainable performance improvement.

Overview of the process:

- **Clarify priorities:** Define how the problem or opportunity fits into your strategic mission, what the desired outcomes are, what success should look like, and how to create alignment with strategic priorities.
- **Conduct a root-cause analysis:** Address the question of what the current performance problem is, what factors created it, and what an effective desired outcome looks like.
- **Define key roles, stakeholders, and actions to build commitment:** Lasting change comes from a coalition of stakeholders. Identify clients, sponsors, and key stakeholders, and determine their level of commitment to change.
- **Create a project plan:** Identify timelines, trade-offs, action steps, key resources and dependencies, potential risks and mitigation. Define shared responsibilities, expectations and clarity regarding how success will be measured.
- **Implement defined solution(s):** Keep stakeholders informed, identify key trade-offs, and be clear about what, why, how, and when each player contributes to change.
- **Measure outcomes:** Based upon agreed-to success criteria from the first step, capture data to tell the story of results achieved. Define what is needed to sustain success.
- **Conduct an after-action review:** Capture learnings from the initiative and use them to improve in the future.

Engaging in a human performance improvement project can solve organizational problems more effectively, build traction, and create productive win/win relationships.

Innovation

The evolution of technology alongside theoretical approaches has spawned innovations in the learning space. Because we have access to a plethora of resources, there will be new methods, products, applications, and tools every day in the learning space. These novelties become innovations when they improve existing conditions, when they enable us to do something better than we have done in the past, and when they add value to our learning experiences.

The terms in this book that fall under the category of innovation are not all-encompassing and may be old news within a matter of months. We opted to include innovations that are familiar to most readers, as we feel that these innovations are the ones that will have the strongest impact on the future landscape of learning.

Terms in this section:

- Augmented Reality
- Machine Learning
- Makerspace
- Predictive Learning Analytics
- Simulation
- Virtual Reality

Shane Santiago
Augmented Reality

What is it?
A full 360-degree digital environment that merges interactive 3D digital assets, along with audio and *haptic feedback*, with your real-world environment. Augmented reality overlays a virtual experience with the real environment, for example, allowing you to view an item in the real world with an explanation virtually overlaid.

Why is it important?
Augmented Reality (AR) gives you the ability to have a *virtual presence* anywhere and share 3D assets through a headset, mobile device, or computer.

Organizations use AR for recruitment, on-boarding, learning, insurance, and marketing; safe handling of dangerous objects; and to bring objects from the past into the present. Many mobile devices contain *LIDAR* technology making it possible to create digital 3D assets on the fly.

About Shane Santiago
Shane oversees creative, strategy and implementation at Bravely. Shane has brought big ideas to world-renowned brands like Marriott International, Johnson & Johnson, The Jacksonville Jaguars, Under Armour, Disney, Discovery, the NBA, Discovery Channel, Paramount Pictures, and Sony Pictures. He's been published in top industry publications, such as Advertising Age, ADWEEK, Communication Arts, and Mashable. Shane earned his BS in advertising at the University of Florida and has served as chair of the University's Advertising Advisory Council. Shane also spent time as the Chair of the American Advertising Federation's National Innovation Committee (NIC).

Email   shane.santiago@bravelycreated.com
Website   bravelycreated.com

Why does a business professional need to know this?

As they have done with most technologies, younger learners in K12 and higher education have embraced AR technology and are using it in their classrooms as an educational tool and also as a way to socialize with each other. It's a glimpse into how your future workforce will communicate, team-build, collaborate, and pass on knowledge.

As a marketing tool, AR goes beyond *consumerism*. You can use it to share your mission statement with your workforce and to create employee *evangelism* within your organization, and it can even help with things like social responsibility and company sustainability efforts.

AR can be used as a powerful storytelling tool that can improve KPIs (Key Performance Indicators) through empathy, and it can even supercharge your employee training in industries such as medicine, education, advertising, healthcare, retail, construction, film, journalism, travel, art, home DIY, automotive, farming, food, and many more. There is literally not a single industry out there that AR couldn't help.

The technology is changing how we interact with employees, but it's also changing how brands interact with their customers and even changing *B2B interactions*.

As a new generation of employees enters the workforce, organizations should be prepared to understand how virtual tools like AR play a role not only in their education efforts but also in the way employees socialize. You need to be current with technology if you want to hold on to your new hires and be competitive in your industry.

Augmented reality is a companion technology to *virtual reality (VR)* and *mixed reality (MR)*.

W. Duncan Welder IV
Machine Learning

What is it?

The science of making machines intelligent through automated data analysis and model building in a way that requires little human oversight. This type of artificial intelligence (AI) is based on the idea that computers can learn to make better decisions through the analysis of data.

Why is it important?

So why is machine learning important today? You are likely interacting with systems using it already. *Voice-to-text* processing uses machine learning to improve based on the way you speak. Amazon uses machine learning to recommend products, and your email is likely using machine learning to identify spam mail. The rapid expansion of computer power and *big data processing* has made machine learning accessible for the masses, including the learning and development industry.

About W. Duncan Welder IV

Duncan Welder holds a master's degree in educational technology and has more than 20 years experience implementing solutions, domestically and abroad. Duncan, an xAPI enthusiast, is passionate about leveraging data to personalize the learning experience. He presents regularly at industry conferences on learning standards.

Duncan has held faculty positions at Bowling Green State University, Ohio, and the College of the Mainland, Texas. He has been published in Learning Solutions, Training Magazine, and US Business Review.

Email   duncanw@risc-inc.com
Twitter   @duncanwiv
LinkedIn linkedin.com/in/duncanwiv/

Why does a business professional need to know this?

Machine learning involves the processing of data to help a computer make better and better decisions. Amazon recommending a product based on your past purchases and your email application determining if a message is spam are both examples of machine learning.

Machine learning is all around us. Business professionals need to understand the potential of machine learning. The development of systems that employ machine learning is complex and requires data scientists with an understanding of *data modeling* and *algorithms*.

Instead of focusing on the technical, consider potential solutions. If banks use machine learning to identify clients with high financial risk, can you leverage similar analysis to head off potential dropouts with an early, personalized learning intervention? If transportation companies use machine learning to outline the most efficient route for delivery drivers, can you use machine learning to optimize your work processes?

With additional automation, it is easy to draw your focus away from the end user who benefits from the new process or system. Business professionals must keep in mind data privacy and *cyber security*. Adhering to industry best practices and clearly communicating how an employee's data is being used are both critical to minimizing the risk of a data leak and maintaining the trust of employees.

A final warning to keep in mind is that machine learning has the potential for bias. Bias is an incorrect assumption in the learning algorithm that can skew results. Review and validation are critical to minimizing the potential for bias.

Donna Marie Andress
Makerspace

What is it?
Risk-free, hands-on learning environments that provide materials, tools, technologies, and support services for learners to transform ideas into projects and products.

Why is it important?
Typically set in physical locations, makerspaces foster curiosity and creativity by enabling participants to learn by doing. Consider what it means to tinker—to explore what you have on hand, see how things might fit together, and try your hand at creating something.

Makerspaces provide that opportunity to tinker—individually and collaboratively—and share our insights along the way. They establish risk-free environments that leverage everything good that comes from giving learners agency to initiate their own learning processes and determine their own pathways to success (or failure).

About Donna Marie Andress
Donna Marie Andress has been teaching & learning for nearly 40 years. Passionate about tech integration and professional development (PD), she is a retired member of the Saratoga Springs City School District, where she was a 16-year veteran of the classroom, then moved into the role of Educational Technology Specialist. For 18 years, Donna worked directly with teachers and students, designed PD courses, wrote documentation, produced training videos, and assisted with systems management. She has also been a certified Microsoft Innovative Educator (MIE) & MIE Master Trainer and a Technology Test Kitchen Chef. Donna is currently a contract trainer and instructional designer with Instructure.

Email   dmandressIT@gmail.com
Twitter   @andressIT
LinkedIn   linkedin.com/in/dmandress153/

Why does a business professional need to know this?

Business professionals can use makerspaces to create environments where employees can envision, prototype, and create business solutions. And employees can participate in some of the many makerspaces that have been created as part of this movement[136].

Key questions to consider that can guide the impact of a makerspace on your organization:

- **Challenge**: What do you want your learners to walk away with?
- **Process**: What steps do they need to take in order to meet the challenge?
- **Resources**: What tools and parts will they need to make their designs happen?
- **Guidance**: What expertise needs to be on hand to help learners?
- **Collaboration**: What opportunities will learners have to collaborate?
- **Safety**: What precautions can you put in place at each stage of the making process to allow learners to safely fail, iterate, re-make, and innovate?
- **Showcase**: Where will you showcase the makerspace products?
- **Conversation**: How will you continue the conversation and continue to engage the community?

A makerspace is not just about making—it's about sharing, modifying, iterating, failing, and re-making. We need more spaces (in-person and virtual) where we can do just that. Many of us learn best by doing, and we need more spaces in our work where we have opportunities to try, and maybe even fail.

Most makerspaces that serve the DIY and builder movements put safety first. This is how, and why failure is ok—nobody gets hurt! Failure can result in iteration, and iteration can result in innovation.

New theories, new practices, and new approaches unveiled in makerspaces can spawn innovations that can shape the future of the business.

Ken Phillips
Predictive Learning Analytics

What is it?

A methodology for pinpointing the underlying causes of *scrap learning* associated with a training program using five key metrics.

Why is it important?

Ensuring a positive return, of both time and money, on a training program is of utmost concern to C-level executives. It should be of equal interest to business professionals concerned about training. However, research indicates that the amount of time and money wasted on training programs is 45–85%[158]. This gap between training delivered, but not applied, is known as scrap learning—the flipside of *training transfer*. Regardless of the percentage, scrap learning is a critical business issue because it wastes time and money.

About Ken Phillips

Ken Phillips is founder and CEO of Phillips Associates and the creator of the Predictive Learning Analytics(PLA) learning evaluation methodology. He has more than 30 years of experience designing learning instruments and assessments and has authored more than a dozen published learning instruments. He regularly speaks to Association for Talent Development (ATD) groups, university classes, and corporate Learning and Development groups. Since 2008 he has presented at the ATD International Conference and Expo and since 2013 at the Annual Training Conference and Expo on topics related to measurement and evaluation of learning. Ken also is a contributing author to five books in the Learning and Development field.

Email	ken@phillipsassociates.com
LinkedIn	linkedin.com/in/ken-phillips-3420b11/

Why does a business professional need to know this?

Decisions based on opinion, intuition, and gut feeling are no longer in vogue. Data-driven decision making is the new norm. Predictive learning analytics, and its use of data to pinpoint the underlying causes of scrap learning associated with a training program, is part of this new norm.

Scrap learning, or the difference between training delivered but not applied back on the job, has been around forever. Scrap learning is the three-thousand-pound elephant in the room whenever business executives and learning professionals engage in a discussion about using a particular solution to address a performance gap or need. It's the elephant in the room because both the business executive and learning professional are fully aware that scrap learning exists. However, neither one wants to talk about it because, previously, there has never been a way to measure, monitor, and manage it.

Consider the effect scrap learning has on an organization's average per-employee training expenditure and the average number of training hours consumed per employee. According to the Association for Talent Development's 2019 State of the Industry Report, in 2018, the average organization spent $1,299 per employee on training[158]. And the average employee spent 34 hours in training. When 45% or more of that is wasted, it is easy to see how much scrap learning costs the average company.

Predictive learning analytics offers a solution to cut this waste by using data to pinpoint its underlying causes[157][156].

Neal Rowland
Simulation

What is it?
The re-creation of a situation, process, or experience to allow a learner to imitate, reproduce, or practice behaviors or actions.

Why is it important?
Learning the proper actions and behaviors required in a particular situation before facing that situation in real life could be the difference between success and failure. Replicating a similar situation is a means for learning and exploration in a cost-effective, safe environment. In some cases, simulation may be the only safe way to prepare, practice, and gain mental and muscle memory.

About Neal Rowland
Neal Rowland is the Lead Crowd Surfer for The Crowd Training. Neal coaches organizations in the best practices of agility and product management, including instructional design. He is certified as a Project Management Professional (PMP), Agile [SPC, PMI-ACP, CSM], and ITIL (Information Technology Infrastructure Library). Neal develops and constructs learning content and resources for a variety of topics, industries, and modalities. Incorporating design thinking he merges pedagogical best practices with graphic design, multimedia, and technology.

Email	nealrowland@live.com
Website	thecrowdtraining.com
Twitter	@thecrowdtrain
LinkedIn	linkedin.com/in/neallrowland/

Why does a business professional need to know this?

Humans learn best by doing. Committing something to muscle memory and mental memory takes time and practice. Practice is good, but at the moment it matters, your preparation may not be enough. Applying your practice in realistic situations and conditions is what matters most. Knowing how you or others will apply the knowledge at the moment of need or application relies on many factors and variables.

As a business professional you and your colleagues may face many situations, but how do you know how to act in each situation? Simulation assists in that assessment. Simulation replicates as much as possible the conditional environment and potential variables you might encounter.

Conducted in a safe space without real-life consequences, simulations present situations that allow learners to apply their learning in more depth, considering more inputs. Creating a simulated experience to act and learn from may mean the difference between life and death when a similar situation occurs in real life.

Niall Campion
Virtual Reality

What is it?
Broadly describes any technology that allows users to immerse themselves in a digital world. Its current iteration, typically delivered via a *head-mounted display*, allows users to experience situations that are removed from their physical location.

Why is it important?
Allowing users to immerse themselves in situations removed from their current physical location opens up a myriad of opportunities for the advancement of learning technology. By employing virtual reality in the learning process trainers and instructors now possess the ability to place learners in a training environment that is analogous to a real scenario without exposing them to risk or incurring the expense associated with real-world training.

About Niall Campion
Niall Campion is the founder and managing director of VRAI. Niall's background is as an award-winning editor, director, and visual effects artist working in the film and television industry. Niall specializes in technological innovation to tell stories in a more interesting and engaging way. Niall also has a passion for sustainable business and has played a key role in implementing the Triple Bottom Line accountancy framework at VRAI.

Email   niall@vrai.ie
LinkedIn   linkedin.com/in/niall-vrai/

Why does a business professional need to know this?

Virtual Reality (VR) will increasingly become part of a suite of new technologies that will shape the future of business. Aside from opportunities offered in the training space, it will present new ways of working.

From training to meeting to interfacing with computers in general, virtual reality comes with the promise of a new computing paradigm. Business professionals should know this term as it will increasingly form part of how their organizations operate.

In the learning and development space, virtual reality has the potential to revolutionize how people learn. By taking concepts and technologies that were once the sole preserve of fighter pilots and bringing them to the factory floor, virtual reality offers the potential for deployable simulation training for all.

Virtual reality can be presented in a small, light, and portable form factor via an affordable head-mounted display. These headsets currently track the user's head and hands as they move in the real world in order to enable them to interact with a virtual, computer-generated world in a realistic way.

Virtual reality is a subset of immersive technology which also includes *Augmented Reality (AR)* and *Mixed Reality (MR)*. Immersive technologies can also include non-headset-based options such as *immersive projection rooms* or wrap-around large-scale visual displays.

Glossary of Additional Terms

This glossary contains terms that support the main terms in the book. They include both additional learning terms and business terms that relate to education and training.

affective domain

In Bloom's Taxonomy, the affective domain refers to the learner's reactions, emotions, or feelings. Learning objectives written to address the affective domain specify levels of awareness and growth in attitudes, emotions, and/or feelings, such as characterizing, organizing, valuing, responding, receiving.

algorithms

A set of instructions that define a sequence of actions and decisions to solve a particular problem. An algorithm is a high-level description of how to solve the problem. To use an algorithm, you need to create a computer program that implements the algorithm. (See *adaptive learning* and *machine learning*)

alt text

Also, alternative text. Supplemental text added to content (typically an image) that describes that content. Used by rendering systems when the content cannot be rendered or when a user is unable to view the content in its original form. (See *accessibility*)

assessor

Someone who is knowledgeable in a particular field who is asked to provide advice, possibly to judge competency in that field. (See *certification*)

authentic learning

Learning content and methods focused on connecting learning with real-world issues, problems, and applications experienced on the job. (See *blended learning*)

autodidactic learner

A person who studies and possibly masters a topic without formal training. Also known as an *autodidact*, an autodidactic learner decides what to study, seeks out resources, determines the best way to learn a new topic, and implements a course of action to gain the desired level of proficiency. (See *heutagogy*)

B2B interactions

Business-to-Business transaction of any type. It could be one business exchanging goods for services from the other or one business purchasing products from another at wholesale pricing. (See *augmented reality*)

benchmark standards

A reference used to compare or evaluate performance. For example, a company may set an a sales benchmark for how many sales are closed in a particular time interval.

big data processing

The extraction and processing of large volumes of information (data) for use in supporting decisions, solving problems, or predicting behaviors or outcomes. (See *machine learning*)

co-learning

Working in groups to share knowledge and resources. Also known as collaborative learning.

code of ethics

An individual's personal values and sense of right and wrong. Also, a set of standards of conduct that members of a group are expected to uphold. (See *certification*)

cognitive domain

In Bloom's Taxonomy, the cognitive domain refers to the level of knowledge attained. Learning objectives written to address the cognitive domain include: evaluation, synthesis (or creation), analysis, application, comprehension, knowledge.

cognitive tests

An assessment of a person's thinking ability. An IQ test is an example of a cognitive test.

collaborative social technologies

Technologies or tools that exist to make it possible for people to seek out help, share best practices, and collaborate with others, whether in real time or asynchronously. These technologies make it easier to offer and receive advice, instructions, corrections etc. (See *blended learning*)

consumerism

Social and economic systems set up to encourage people to keep buying goods and services, especially those they likely don't even need, in ever-increasing amounts. (See *augmented reality*)

contrast ratio

A property of a display expressed as the ratio of the luminance of the brightest shade to that of the darkest shade that the display is capable of rendering. Accessible content will use a high contrast ratio. (See *accessibility*)

critical pedagogy

A philosophy of education developed to encompass culture, social justice, and democracy as integral elements of education. (See *pedagogy*)

critical thinking

Application and analysis of facts to form reasoned judgement.

customer relationship management (CRM)

A process in which an organization maintains records of all interactions with customers. The information is then used for data analysis (aka data mining) to look for customer preferences, trends, etc.

cybersecurity

The art of protecting networks, devices, and data from unauthorized access or criminal use and the practice of ensuring confidentiality, integrity, and availability of information. Definition from the US Cybersecurity and Infrastructure Security Agency (CISA). (See *machine learning*)

data analytics

The practice of formulating and reporting insights derived from data. (See *adaptive learning*)

data modeling

Analysts use information (data) to build models that are used to predict possible behaviors and outcomes. (See *machine learning*)

design system

Set of related patterns and shared practices arranged or organized for use in streamlining digital content. (See *learning environment modeling*)

didactic

Example intended to teach with an ulterior motive that is likely based on a moral topic or instruction. (See *andragogy*)

dissemination methodologies

The way or ways that content will be shared or distributed to learners.

distractor answers

The incorrect answers offered in a multiple-choice test question.

domain-specific knowledge

Knowledge in a specific discipline. Several theorists have put forward theories that claim that we each have more than one type of independent or specialized knowledge structure or domain. (See *communities of practice*)

e-portfolio

Digital evidence of someone's work product stored and maintained on the web. Also known as an electronic portfolio. (See *digital badges*)

environmental stimuli

Our senses recognize and respond, both consciously and unconsciously, to things taking place around us all of the time. Environmental stimuli help to embed learning in our brains and make it available for recall. Examples include: temperature changes, weather, humidity, heat, cold, smells, tastes, level of comfort, sounds, noises, etc. (See *behaviorism*)

evangelism

A zealous advocacy of something, especially a cause or product. (See *augmented reality*)

extrinsic motivation

Completion of an activity because it is required or carries with it some form of external reward.

fab lab

A workshop where people can fabricate nearly anything that can be made using 3D printing or machining equipment. Groups are provided fabrication equipment they can use to build whatever they can dream up. (See *Makerspace*)

game aesthetics

Elements that make up the user interface (UI) for the game, setting the scene and providing both context and ease of use. Game aesthetics includes things like: locations, color combinations, button placement, labels, sounds, etc.

game dynamics

Specifications as to how a game encourages players to engage with the game and continue to participate. This is sometimes referred to as the user experience (UX). Game dynamics includes things like:

types of social interaction and elements, companion avatar(s), level of difficulty, feedback, how quickly or slowly players are able to achieve success, etc.

game elements

The rules and procedures that define how to play a game and achieve levels of mastery. (See *gamification*)

game mechanics

Specifications as to how a game will be played. Game mechanics includes things like: single player or multi-player game, number of levels of achievement, point systems, quizzes, distractors, etc.

game thinking

Amy Jo Kim defines game thinking this way: "Game Thinking is the art and science of engaging customers on a compelling path to mastery." (See *gamification*)

gamify

See *gamification, game-based learning,* and *digital badges.*

hackerspace

Gatherings of people with similar interests, typically computers or technology, to work on projects, share ideas, and socialize. (See *Makerspace*)

haptic feedback

Technology that creates an experience (e.g., providing feedback or acceptance of commands) through touch, vibration, or movement. (See *augmented reality*)

head-mounted display

Part of a helmet or other type of headwear that is worn when interacting with virtual reality simulations and experiences. (See *virtual reality*)

higher-order thinking levels

Bloom's Taxonomy qualifies thinking skills as lower order and higher order. Higher-order thinking skills require someone to use more than their memory to recall and apply something. Higher-order thinking skills include: analyzing, evaluating, and creating.

human-centered design

An approach to designing learning that takes people's behaviors, preferences, and pain points into account to help them find the best ways to creatively solve problems. (See *learning experience design*)

immersive projection rooms
An immersive learning environment that uses projection on the walls, floor, and ceiling, possibly in combination with movement, touch, scent, and sound, to provide a learning experience. (See *virtual reality*)

implicit learning propensity
Ability to learn organically in one's own environment without setting the intention to learn.

intrinsic motivation
Completing an activity for the pure satisfaction of having accomplished that activity.

item analysis
A process of analyzing learner responses to questions in an assessment in order to validate the overall quality of the assessment. This includes an analysis of question difficulty, distribution of scoring, and the value of *distractor answers*.

journey maps
A series of user or learner visualizations or actions mapped to a timeline. (See *learning experience design*)

knowledge management
Process of creating, sharing, using, and managing the organization's knowledge and information and used as the basis for learning within the organization. (See *communities of practice*)

learning and development infrastructure
An organizational framework constructed to support the development, management, and delivery of learning content. This includes the systems, policies, procedures, and personnel devoted to learning and development. (See *coaching*)

learning campaign
A long-term plan for embedding learning. Learning campaigns employ a variety of methods. (See *blended learning*)

learning strategy
A method or methods learners use to learn. May also refer to a broader strategy employed by a company for its overall learning and development work. (See *adaptive learning*, *evaluation*, and *pedagogy*)

learning style

The idea that individuals differ with respect to what modes of instruction are most effective for them. While learners do have *preferences* regarding how they learn material (see *learner preference*) there is little evidence that instruction that is tailored to a particular *style* makes a significant difference in learning outcomes[112]. (See *learner preference*)

licensure

The granting of a license to perform an activity or profession or to hold a particular title. Many careers require you to obtain a license to practice, which is conferred by an authorized regulating authority. (See *accreditation* and *certification*)

LIDAR

Method used to determine the distance to an object by targeting the object with a laser and then measuring the time for the reflected light to return to the receiver. LIDAR is an acronym for either: "LIght Detection And Ranging" or "Laser Imaging, Detection, And Ranging." (See *augmented reality*)

long-term memory

The area of our brains that retains information and stimuli over long periods of time. (See *cognitivism*)

lower-order thinking levels

Bloom's Taxonomy qualifies thinking skills as lower order and higher order. Lower-order thinking skills are applied when someone uses memory and basic knowledge to recall something. Lower-order thinking skills include: remembering, understanding, and applying.

Massive Open Online Course (MOOC)

A free, online course that anyone can take. (See *open educational resources*)

measurable behaviors

Many behaviors are measurable in some way. In the learning and development context, the instructional design team strives to define what is measurable, the criteria for measuring behavior, and how best to measure it. This information helps them write performance objectives. (See *behaviorism*)

mental structures

Behaviors, thoughts, ideas, or systems used by an individual to establish a basis for recognizing and assimilating new information. (See *constructivism*)

metacognition
Awareness of one's own learning and thinking patterns.

metacognitive learning
Awareness and regulation of one's own thoughts and the ability to change them.

micro-credential
Acknowledgement of an achievement usually characterized by having a short completion time and covering a narrow subject area. Learners explore and complete learning activities in a small area of knowledge, then prove their competence to be conferred a micro-certification or micro-credential. (See *digital badges*)

mixed reality
An immersive learning environment that combines physical elements or experiences with virtual reality elements or experiences. (See *augmented reality* and *virtual reality*)

moment of learning need
A point where there is a need for training. Research conducted by Conrad Gottfredson and Bob Mosher identified five unique moments when people are learning, especially with respect to learning on the job. They define them this way: learn new, learn more, apply, solve, change. The first two are associated with formal learning events and the last three are associated with performance support while working. (See *blended learning*)

open access
Initiatives that remove paywalls and other barriers to accessing academic and scientific resources. Open access refers to a wide variety of initiatives that use different models that are aimed at making research available without charge to readers. Open access does not address the question of copyright. *Open educational resources (OER)* refers to educational resources that are licensed under copyright terms, typically Creative Commons, that allow materials to be used and re-purposed.

open pedagogy
Form of experiential learning where the learners demonstrate their level of skill or knowledge by creating information, rather than simply being consumers of it. (See *pedagogy*)

operant conditioning
A learning where desirable behavior is reinforced or rewarded and undesirable behavior is punished. (See *social and informal learning*)

performance support
Refers to any tool that helps people apply a skill, solve a problem, or complete a task while on the job. (See *Assessment, delivery mode,* and *instructional design*)

personal learning paths
The way that a learner chooses to learn content to meet their personal objectives. Learners craft their own learning goals, decide how they prefer to learn, and determine how they will assess their knowledge of the content. (See *blended learning*)

personas
Fictitious characters created to help user-experience designers understand who consumes their content and uses their interfaces. Personas provide designers with concrete examples of people who might use their products, using characteristics such as age, sex, background, interests, etc. (See *learning experience design*)

portfolio
A collection of work compiled to showcase sets of skills and achievements.

progressive learning
A method of teaching that emphasizes teaching students how to think rather than teaching facts. Also referred to as progressive education[92]. (See *game-based learning*)

prototypes
An explanatory mockup of a proposed solution. Prototypes are used to test the feasibility and usability of a system before committing to a full implementation. (See *learning experience design*)

question analysis
A statistical method for evaluating the overall performance and quality of questions in an assessment in order to identify questions that do not align with learner performance.

reflective analysis
An opportunity to reflect and analyze one's experience as it relates to the goals and expectations for the learning.

ROI
Return on Investment. The ratio between the amount spent on a project or investment and the value that project or investment yields. *assessment*)

SCORM

Shareable Content Object Reference Model. A set of standards that define communication between a *learning management system (LMS)* and a client system delivering training to a student.

scrap learning

The amount of training delivered but never applied back on the job. Scrap learning is a measure of wasted training resources and learning time. (See *predictive analytics*)

screen reader

Assistive technology used by those who are visually impaired, blind, or with low reading ability. A screen reader renders onscreen text and the alt text for images using a reading voice or Braille. (See *accessibility*)

semantic markup

Markup, typically XML, that defines the *meaning* of an element rather than its visual representation. For example, the HTML element <em> tells a web browser to emphasize text, but does not specify how to visually represent the text. You can then use CSS to specify how you want <em> to be rendered. The HTML element <i>, on the other hand, specifies an italic font face. Using semantic markup, like the <em> element, makes it easy for you to change aspects of style without touching the source content. (See *accessibility*)

sensory domain

In Bloom's Taxonomy, the sensory domain (also know as the sensory domain) is the action-based domain. Learning objectives written to address the sensory domain specify levels of learning through the use of words such as origination, adaptation, complex overt response, mechanism, guided response, set, perception.

service design

An activity undertaken to plan and arrange people, infrastructure, communication, or material to improve quality and/or intersection between the element(s) and its users. (See *learning experience design*)

short-term memory

A holding area in a person's memory used for retaining information for short periods of time. The brain then sorts and files this information and, as needed. stores in longer term memory. This holding area is also called "primary" or "active" memory. (See *working memory*)

situated learning

Learning that occurs in the same environment that the learned skills are practiced. An example is on-the-job training that takes place in the workplace. (See *constructivism*)

Software as a Service (SaaS)

A software licensing and delivery subscription model where software is hosted on a central server and used through an app or web browser. May also be referred to as on-demand software.

stacked badges

A badge is an indicator that someone has achieved some goal. Badges figure prominently in many environments, but especially in gamified environments. Stacked badges can be thought of as a sequence of badges that represent ever-increasing levels of accomplishment. (See *digital badges*)

standardized tests

Any test administered in the same manner to all who take the test. Standardized tests are also graded in the same manner for everyone who took the test.

tacit knowledge

A person's skills, ideas, or experiences that they would find difficult to state how or where they learned them. This knowledge likely can only be revealed through continuous practice or repetition in a particular context. This is sometimes referred to as *informal learning*.

training transfer

The ability of learners to apply knowledge and skills acquired through training to their work. (See *Microlearning* and *predictive analytics*)

usability research

Quality measures that assess how users experience content or an interface and where they encounter difficulties. (See *learning experience design*)

user experience (UX) design

The practice of designing digital content to be more usable and useful for those using the interface. (See *learning experience design*)

user research

Analysis of expected consumers, including their points of pain, in order to ensure that the best content is designed to best meet their needs. (See *learning experience design*)

virtual presence

Immersive simulation, virtual reality (VR), or augmented reality (AR) provides users with a sensory experience where they feel as though they are actually in the virtual location. (See *augmented reality*)

voice-to-text

Speech recognition technology used to transform spoken words into written text or to deliver commands to a computer application. (See *machine learning*)

working memory

The area of our short-term memory that is primarily devoted to immediate, conscious processing. (See *cognitive load, cognitivism* and *working memory*)

References

Accessibility by Char James-Tanny

[1] *Web Content Accessibility Guidelines (WCAG) 2.1*
https://www.w3.org/TR/WCAG21/
World Wide Web Consortium. (June 5 2018). A set of recommendations for making content on the web more accessible. Includes success criteria for meeting the guidelines.

[2] *WebAIM: Web Accessibility in Mind*
http://webaim.org/
Articles, blog, newsletter, and discussion lists.

[3] *International Web Accessibility Laws and Policies*
https://www.whoisaccessible.com/guidelines/international-web-accessibility-laws-and-policies/
Akinyemi, Adam. (July 2020). Accessibility laws by country.

[4] *Center for Disease Control and Prevention: Disability Impacts All of Us*
https://www.cdc.gov/ncbddd/disabilityandhealth/infographic-disability-impacts-all.html
Centers for Disease Control and Prevention. Infographic showing how everyone is affected by disabilities in one way or another.

[5] *Design Delight from Disability - 2020 Annual Report: The Global Economics of Disability*
http://rod-group.com/content/rod-research/edit-research-design-delight-disability-2020-annual-report-global-economics
Donovan, Rich. (2020). The Return on Disability Group.

Accreditation by Karan Powell

[6] *Accreditation: Postsecondary Education Institutions*
https://www.ed.gov/accreditation
US Department of Education. Site contains links to US government information on accredited institutions and the accreditation process.

[7] *Council for Higher Education Accreditation*
https://www.chea.org/
CHEA. Web site for the organization, which focuses on higher education accreditation and quality assurance.

[8] *The Value of Accreditation*
https://www.acpe-accredit.org/pdf/ValueofAccreditation.pdf
Council for Higher Education Accreditation (CHEA). (2021). PDF article.

[9] *What is Accreditation?*
https://www.worldwidelearn.com/accreditation/
World-wide Learn. Descriptions of accreditation, including types of accreditation and accreditation organizations.

[10] *Regulatory Resources*
https://www.iacet.org/resources/regulatory-resources/
International Accreditors for Continuing Education (IACET). Information about the IACET, which is an organization to promote accreditation.

Adaptive Learning by JD Dillon

[11] *7 Things You Should Know About Adaptive Learning*
https://library.educause.edu/resources/2017/1/7-things-you-should-know-about-adaptive-learning
Moskal, Patsy, Don Carter, and Dale Johnson. (2017). EDUCAUSE Learning Initiative, 2017. Web page with downloadable PDF.

[12] *Adaptive Learning: How Technology Is Breaking Down Barriers In Education*
https://www.forbes.com/sites/forbestechcouncil/2021/05/21/adaptive-learning-how-technology-is-breaking-down-barriers-in-education/
Alexander, Steve. (2021). Forbes.

[13] *Adaptive Learning is the Future of Education. Are Education Networks Ready?*
https://www.ciena.com/insights/articles/adaptive-learning-future-education-collaboration-edtech-networks.html
Loffreda, Daniele. (2021). Ciena.

Andragogy by Alexandra Pickett

[14] *The e-mature learner*
https://webarchive.nationalarchives.gov.uk/20080806221011/http://tre.ngfl.gov.uk/uploads/materials/24875/
The_emature_learner_John_Anderson.doc
Anderson, John (2006). edited by Janice Staines. Microsoft Word file. Think-piece for the British Educational Communications Technology Agency (Becta). Archived by the UK Government Web Archive.

[15] *A Simple, Easy to Understand Guide to Andragogy*
https://www.cornerstone.edu/blog-post/a-simple-easy-to-understand-guide-to-andragogy/
Graham, Steve. (2017). Lifelong Learning Matters, Cornerstone University.

[16] *Andragogy Theory — Malcolm Knowles*
https://educationaltechnology.net/andragogy-theory-malcolm-knowles/
Kurt, Serhat. (2020). In Educational Technology, June 30, 2020.

Assessment by Myra Travin

[17] *Assessment*
https://www.edutopia.org/assessment
Edutopia. George Lucas Educational Foundation. Website that points to
a group of web articles about assessment.

[18] *Measuring student learning*
https://teaching.cornell.edu/teaching-resources/assessment-evaluation/
measuring-student-learning
Center for Teaching Innovation. Cornell University.

[19] *The Importance of Summative and Formative Assessments Within a Training
Program*
https://teaching.cornell.edu/teaching-resources/assessment-evaluation/
measuring-student-learning
Newey, Marty. (2019). AllenComm blog.

[20] *Understanding Formative Assessment: Insights from Learning Theory and
Measurement Theory*
https://www2.wested.org/www-static/online_pubs/resource1307.pdf
Trumbull, Elise, and Andrea Lash. (2013). WestEd. PDF format.

Augmented Reality by Shane Santiago

[21] *How Augmented Reality Works*
https://computer.howstuffworks.com/augmented-reality.htm
Bonsor, Kevin, and Nathan Chandler. How Stuff Works.

[22] *3 Ways Augmented Reality is Modernizing Employee Training*
https://www.ptc.com/en/blogs/ar/3-ways-augmented-reality-is-
modernizing-employee-training
Kaminsky, Greg. (2020). PTC.

[23] *7 Augmented Reality Tools for the Classroom*
https://www.edutopia.org/article/7-augmented-reality-tools-classroom
Danhoff, Christine. (2021). Edutopia, George Lucas Educational Foundation.

[24] *Augmented Reality in Learning: What is AR and How Will it Revolutionise
Training?*
https://www.growthengineering.co.uk/augmented-reality-learning/
Growth Engineering. (2020).

[25] *The Benefits Of Augmented Reality For Employee Training*
https://www.forbes.com/sites/forbesbusinesscouncil/2021/02/12/the-
benefits-of-augmented-reality-for-employee-training/
Fade, Lorne. (2021). Forbes.

Behaviorism by Jillian Powers

[26] *Behaviorist Approach*
https://www.simplypsychology.org/behaviorism.html
McLeod, Saul. (2020 update). Simply Psychology.

[27] *Behaviorism*
https://iep.utm.edu/behaviorism/
Hauser, Larry. Internet Encyclopedia of Philosophy

[28] *Which Learning Theories are Right for Your Organization?*
https://www.learnupon.com/blog/learning-theories/
Lawless, Caroline. (2019). LearnUpon Blog

Blended Learning by Jennifer Hofmann

[29] *Blended Learning*
https://www.td.org/books/blended-learning
Hoffman, Jennifer. (February 2018). Association for Talent Development.
ISBN: 978-1-562860981.

[30] *Blended Learning Built on Teacher Expertise*
https://www.edutopia.org/article/blended-learning-built-teacher-expertise
Farah, Kareem. (May 2019). Edutopia, George Lucas Educational
Foundation.

Bloom's Taxonomy by Joy Adams

[31] *Bloom's Taxonomy*
https://cft.vanderbilt.edu/guides-sub-pages/blooms-taxonomy/
Armstrong, Patricia. (2010). Vanderbilt University Center for Teaching.
Retrieved July 22, 2022.

[32] *Bloom beyond Bloom: Using the Revised Taxonomy to develop experiential
learning strategies*
https://elearningindustry.com/blooms-taxonomy-for-business-use
Flanagan, Deanna. (2019). How to Use Bloom's Taxonomy for Business.
Retrieved July 22, 2022.

[33] *A Revision of Bloom's Taxonomy: An Overview.*
https://www.depauw.edu/files/resources/krathwohl.pdf
Krathwohl, David R. (2002). *Theory into Practice* 41, 4 (Autumn): 212-
218. PDF format.

[34] *An application of Bloom's Taxonomy to the teaching of business ethics*
https://tips.uark.edu/blooms-taxonomy-verb-chart/
Shabatura, Jessica. (2014). University of Arkansas TIPS (Teaching Innovation and Pedagogical Support).

Certification by Saul Carliner

[35] *Chartered Institute for Personnel and Development (CIPD)*
https://www.cipd.org/en/
Well-respected professional organization devoted to human resources
and development of people.

[36] *Society for Human Resource Management (SHRM)*
https://www.shrm.org/certification/
Organization that offers the SHRM-CP (certified professional) and
SHRM-SCP (senior certified professional) certifications.

[37] *ATD Certified Professional in Talent Development (CPTD)*
https://www.td.org/certification/cptd/introduction
Certification offered by the Association for Talent Development (ATP).

[38] *ISPI Certified Performance Technologist (CPT)*
https://ispi.org/page/CPTStandards
Certification offered by International Society for Performance Improvement (ISPI).

[39] *CompTIA Certified Technical Trainer (CTT+)*
https://www.comptia.org/certifications/ctt
Certification offered by the Computing Technology Industry Association
(CompTIA).

Coaching by Vincent Han

[40] *The Leader as Coach*
https://hbr.org/2019/11/the-leader-as-coach
Ibarra, Herminia, and Anne Scoular. (2019). Harvard Business Review,
November-December 2019. Behind paywall that allows limited free access
(two articles per month).

[41] *Using Coaching to Develop Olympian Employees*
https://trainingindustry.com/articles/strategy-alignment-and-planning/
using-coaching-to-develop-olympian-employees/
Oesch, Taryn. (2019). Training Industry.

[42] *Coaching employees to reach optimal performance*
https://www2.deloitte.com/us/en/pages/human-capital/articles/coaching-
employees-to-reach-optimal-performance.html
Deloitte. (2020).

Cognitive Load by Phylise Banner

[43] *Cognitive-Load Theory: Methods to Manage Working Memory Load in the Learning of Complex Tasks*
https://journals.sagepub.com/doi/full/10.1177/0963721420922183
Paas, Fred, and Jeroen J. G. van Merriënboer. *Current Directions in Psychological Science* 29, no. 4, (Aug. 2020): 394-398.

[44] *Your Guide To Cognitive Load Theory And Learning*
https://www.edgepointlearning.com/blog/cognitive-load-theory-and-learning/
Bleich, Corey. (2019). Edgepoint Learning.

[45] *Tips To Avoid Cognitive Overload In Employee Training Programs*
https://elearningindustry.com/avoid-cognitive-overload-in-employee-training-programs
Hughes, Andrew. (December 2019). eLearning Industry.

[46] *Efficiency in Learning: Evidence-Based Guidelines to Manage Cognitive Load*
Clark, Ruth C., Frank Nguyen, and John Sweller. (2005). Pfeiffer. ISBN: 978-0787977283.

Cognitivism by Ashley Reardon

[47] *Cognitivism*
https://edtechbooks.org/studentguide/cognitivism
Michela, Esther. (2018). In *The Student's Guide to Learning Design and Research*. EdTech Books.

[48] *Cognitivism*
https://pressbooks.bccampus.ca/teachinginadigitalagev2/chapter/3-3-cognitivism/
Bates, A. W. (Tony). (2019). In *Teaching in a Digital Age*. 2nd ed. British Columbia/Yukon Open Authoring Platform. Open source textbook.

[49] *Implications Of Learning Theories On Instructional Design*
https://elearningindustry.com/learning-theories-instructional-design-implications
Reynolds, Jon-Erik. (March 2018). eLearning Industry.

Communities of Practice by Rhoda Deon

[50] *Cultivating Communities of Practice: a Guide to Managing Knowledge—Seven Principles for Cultivating Communities of Practice.*
https://hbswk.hbs.edu/archive/cultivating-communities-of-practice-a-guide-to-managing-knowledge-seven-principles-for-cultivating-communities-of-practice
Wenger, Etienne, Richard McDermott, and William Snyder. (March 2002). Harvard Business Review Press.

[51] *Introduction to Communities of Practice*
https://wenger-trayner.com/introduction-to-communities-of-practice/
Wenger-Trayner, Etienne, and Beverly Wenger-Trayner. (2015). PDF
format.

[52] *Communities of Practice*
https://www.youtube.com/watch?v=SmqLyOLIjos
Wenger-Trayner, Etienne. (2022), YouTube video.

[53] *Situated Learning: Legitimate Peripheral Participation*
Lave, Jean, and Etienne Wenger. (1991). Cambridge University Press.
ISBN: 978-0521413084.

Competency-Based Learning by Dan McCann

[54] *The 70-20-10 Rule for Learning and Development*
https://trainingindustry.com/wiki/content-development/the-702010-
model-for-learning-and-development/
Training Industry blog. (2014). Although this model does not have strong
research behind it, it is widely used within the learning community.

[55] *Competency-Based Training: The New Trend in Employee Development*
https://calipercorp.com/blog/competency-based-training-the-new-trend-
in-employee-development/
Allgaier, Andrew. (December 2020). PSI Caliper.

[56] *The Importance Of Competency-Based Learning In Employee Skills Development*
https://elearningindustry.com/competency-based-learning-employee-
skills-development
Janoska, Lubos. (April 2020). eLearning Industry

[57] *The ABC's of Competency-Based Learning*
https://www.shiftelearning.com/blog/the-abc-s-of-competency-based-
learning
Bautista, Jonatan. Shift Learning Blog

[58] *Competency-Based Training Basics*
Rothwell, William J., and James M. Graber. (2010). Association for Talent
Development (ATD). ISBN: 978-1562866983.

Constructivism by Karen Swan

[59] *Constructivist Learning Theory*
https://www.exploratorium.edu/education/ifi/constructivist-learning
Hein, George E. (1991). CECA (International Committee of Museum
Educators) Conference, 15–22 October, 1991.

[60] *Objectivism versus Constructivism: Do we Need a New Philosophical Paradigm?*
https://www.jstor.org/stable/30219973
Jonassen, David H. *Educational Technology Research and Development* 39, no. 3, (1991):5–14. Available through subscription or purchase.

[61] *Constructivism and Instructional Design*
https://www.jstor.org/stable/44427520
Merrill, M. David. *Educational Technology* 31, no. 5 (May 1991):45–53. Available through subscription or purchase.

Curation by David Kelly

[62] *Curation Nation*
https://curationnation.org/
Rosenbaum, Steven. (2011). McGraw-Hill Education. ISBN: 978-0071760393.

[63] *Innovate — curation!*
https://www.youtube.com/watch?v=iASluLoKQbo
Rosenbaum, Steven. (2011). TEDxGrandRapids. YouTube video.

Curriculum by Bryan Alexander

[64] *The Glossary of Education Reform: Curriculum*
https://www.edglossary.org/curriculum/
The Great Schools Partnership.

[65] *Curriculum Definition*
https://www.ride.ri.gov/InstructionAssessment/Curriculum/CurriculumDefinition.aspx
Rhode Island Department of Education.

Delivery Mode by John Vivolo

[66] *Delivery Modes and Teaching Approaches*
https://www.buffalo.edu/catt/develop/design/delivery-modes.html
University of Buffalo Curriculum, Assessment, and Teaching Transformation. Website.

Digital Badges by Chris Price

[67] *The Seven Deadly Sins Of Digital Badging In Education*
https://www.forbes.com/sites/troymarkowitz/2018/09/16/the-seven-deadly-sins-of-digital-badging-in-education-making-badges-student-centered/
Markowitz, Troy. (2018). Forbes.

[68] *The Power of Digital Badges*
https://www.ascd.org/el/articles/the-power-of-digital-badges
Niguidula, David. (2020). ASCD.

[69] *6 Reasons Why Online Course Creators Should Use Digital Badges*
https://elearningindustry.com/why-online-course-creators-use-digital-badges
Weiss, Mike. (2020). eLearning Industry.

[70] *7 Things You Should Know About Digital Badges*
https://library.educause.edu/resources/2019/7/7-things-you-should-know-about-digital-badges
Braxton, Sherri, et al. (2019). EDUCAUSE. Includes links to a downloadable PDF and ePub.

[71] *5 Best Practices in Using Digital Badging for Employee Upskilling and Reskilling*
https://www.gofluent.com/blog/digital-badging-learning-and-development/
De Vera, Tristan. (2021). goFLUENT.

eLearning by Joe Ganci

[72] *Building an Inclusive Definition of E-Learning: An Approach to the Conceptual Framework*
https://files.eric.ed.gov/fulltext/EJ983277.pdf
Sangrà, Albert, Dimitrios Vlachopoulos, and Nati Cabrera. (2012). *The International Review of Research in Open and Distance Learning* 13, no. 2. PDF format. Article is licensed under CC BY 4.0.

Engagement by Kassy LaBorie

[73] *The Glossary of Education Reform*
https://www.edglossary.org/
A perspective from education

[74] *Learners Engagement in Corporate Learning*
https://elearningindustry.com/engagement-in-corporate-training-learners
A blog post from a corporate learning perspective

[75] *How To Motivate Learners: 7 Surefire Learner Engagement Strategies*
https://www.talentlms.com/ebook/learner-engagement/strategies
An eBook focused on learner engagement

[76] *The relationship between learner engagement and teaching effectiveness: a novel assessment of student engagement in continuing medical education*
https://bmcmededuc.biomedcentral.com/articles/10.1186/s12909-020-02331-x
Stephenson, Christopher R. (2020). BMC Medical Education.

[77] *A Comparative Study of Student Engagement, Satisfaction, and Academic Success among International and American Students*
https://files.eric.ed.gov/fulltext/EJ1052833.pdf
Korobova, Nadia. (2015). *Journal of International Students* 5, 1 (2015): 72–85. PDF format.

[78] *Interact and Engage! 75+ Activities for Virtual Training, Meetings, and Webinars, 2nd edition*
https://kassyconsulting.com/book-interact-and-engage-2nd-edition/
LaBorie, Kassy. (2015). ATD Press.

[79] *Producing Virtual Training, Meetings, and Webinars*
https://kassyconsulting.com/book-producing-virtual-training-meetings-and-webinars/
LaBorie, Kassy. (2020). ATD Press.

Evaluation by Alexander Salas

[80] *Evaluating Training Programs: The Four Levels*
Kirkpatrick, Donald L., and James D. Kirkpatrick. (2006). Berrett-Koehler Publishers. ISBN: 978-1576753484.

[81] *The Kirkpatrick Model*
https://www.kirkpatrickpartners.com/the-kirkpatrick-model/
Kirkpatrick Partners. High-level description of the four levels of evaluation.

Experiential Learning by Lorraine Weaver

[82] *A Meta-Analysis of the Relationship Between Experiential Learning and Learning Outcomes*
https://onlinelibrary.wiley.com/doi/10.1111/dsji.12188
Burch, Gerald F., Robert Giambatista, John H. Batchelor, Jana J. Burch, J. Duane Hoover, and Nathan A. Heller. *Decision Sciences Journal of Innovative Education* 17, no. 3 (July 2019):239–273. Subscription or paid download required. This journal article analyzes studies that compared experiential learning activities to traditional learning environments and concludes that learning outcomes are greater when experiential pedagogies are used.

[83] *Outcome-Based Experiential Learning*
https://www.hedbeyond.ca/obel/
Hoessler, Caroline, and Lorraine Godden. (2021). Higher Education and Beyond. ISBN: 978-1777626020. This book is an excellent practical guide for anyone involved in setting-up experiential learning. It provides straightforward guidance relating to a process that can be used to structure the experiential learning as well as identifying specific things that stakeholders should discuss.

[84] *Experiential Learning Theory as a Guide for Experiential Educators in Higher Education*
https://nsuworks.nova.edu/elthe/vol1/iss1/7/
Kolb, Alice Y., and Kolb, David A. *Experiential Learning Theory as a Guide for Experiential Educators in Higher Education* 1 no. 1, Article 7. (2017):7–44. Downloadable in PDF format.

Feedback by Theresa Hummel-Krallinger

[85] *Employee Feedback Is Good For Employee Engagement; Action Is Better*
https://www.forbes.com/sites/deniselyohn/2019/08/06/employee-feedback-is-good-for-employee-engagement-action-is-better/?sh=526aea0974cc

Game-based Learning (GBL) by Marek Hyla

[86] *The Art of Game Design: A Book of Lenses*
Schell, Jesse. (August 2019). A K Peters/CRC Press. 3rd edition. ISBN: 978-1138632059. Great book about designing games with a lot of examples.

[87] *The Gamification of Learning and Instruction: Game-based Methods and Strategies for Training and Education*
https://www.td.org/books/the-gamification-of-learning-and-instruction-game-based-methods-and-strategies-for-training-and-education
Kapp, Karl M. (2012). Wiley. ISBN: 978-1-118-09634-5. Not only about games in learning but also about gamification of learning processes.

[88] *The Game Layer on Top of the World*
https://www.ted.com/talks/seth_priebatsch_the_game_layer_on_top_of_the_world
Priebatsch, Seth. TEDx Boston 2010.

[89] *Latest Game Theory: Mixing Work and Play*
https://www.wsj.com/articles/SB10001424052970204294504576615371783795248
Silverman, Rachel Emma. Wall Street Journal (Oct. 10, 2011). Requires Wall Street Journal subscription.

[90] *How Games Make Kids Smarter*
https://www.ted.com/talks/gabe_zichermann_how_games_make_kids_smarter
Zichermann, Gabe. TEDxKids@Brussels. (June 2011).

[91] *Gaming Can Make a Better World*
https://www.ted.com/talks/jane_mcgonigal_gaming_can_make_a_better_world
McGonigal, Jane. TED2010. (Feb. 2010).

[92] *Progressive Education: How Children Learn*
https://www.thoughtco.com/progressive-education-how-children-learn-today-2774713
Kennedy, Robert. (2019). ThoughtCo. A description of progressive learning.

Gamification by Karl Kapp

[93] *The Gamification of Learning and Instruction Fieldbook: Theory Into Practice*
https://www.td.org/books/the-gamification-fieldbook
Kapp, Karl M. (2013). Wiley. ISBN: 978-1-118-67724-7

[94] *Gamification of Learning*
https://www.linkedin.com/learning/gamification-of-learning
Kapp, Karl M. (2014). LinkedIn training class. Requires subscription or purchase.

[95] *Gamification for Interactive Learning*
https://www.linkedin.com/learning/gamification-for-interactive-learning/gamification-overview
Kapp, Karl M. (2017). LinkedIn training class. Requires subscription or purchase.

[96] *Getting Started with Gamification*
https://www.td.org/insights/getting-started-with-gamification
Kapp, Karl M. (2014). Association for Training Development (ATD). First in a series of three articles on gamifying your instruction. Requires membership in ATD.

[97] *Gamification: Examples and Best Practices in eLearning*
https://www.valamis.com/hub/gamification
Valamis. (2013). Website that defines gamification and provides several examples.

Heutagogy by Bill Pelz

[98] *Heutagogy: It Isn't Your Mother's Pedagogy Any More*
http://nferciindonesia.blogspot.com/2013/04/heutagogy-it-isnt-your-mothers-pedagogy.html
Eberly, Jane, and Marcus Childress. *National Social Science Journal* 28 no. 1 (2007):28–32. While many educators refer to all teaching as pedagogy, this is a term that limits the scope of what teaching can and should be.

Human Performance Improvement by Marjorie Derven

[99] *What is Human Performance Improvement?*
https://www.td.org/insights/what-is-human-performance-improvement
Ross, Chris. (2017). Association for Talent Development.

[100] *Fundamentals of HPI*
https://www.td.org/td-at-work/fundamentals-of-hpi
Association for Talent Development. (1998). Requires subscription or purchase.

[101] *Human Performance Improvement: Keeping an Eye on Results in a World of Wants and Needs*
https://www.hrexchangenetwork.com/learning/articles/human-performance-improvement-keeping-an-eye-on-results-in-a-world-of-wants-and-needs
Rice, David. (2020). HR Exchange Network.

Instructional Design by Dawn Mahoney

[102] *What is Instructional Design?*
https://www.td.org/talent-development-glossary-terms/what-is-instructional-design
Association for Talent Development. Website with a definition of instructional design and links for additional information.

[103] *What is Instructional Design?*
https://online.purdue.edu/blog/education/what-is-instructional-design
Purdue University. Definition of instructional design and information about studying instructional design at Purdue.

[104] *The ADDIE Model for Instructional Design Explained*
https://www.td.org/newsletters/atd-links/all-about-addie
Hodell, Chuck. (2015). Association for Talent Development. Description of the ADDIE model with an explanation of each step in the process.

Interaction by Patrice Torcivia Prusko

[105] *The Impact of Social Interaction on Student Learning*
https://scholarworks.wmich.edu/cgi/viewcontent.cgi?article=3105&context=reading_horizons
Hurst, Beth, Randall Wallace, and Sarah B. Nixon. *Reading Horizons: A Journal of Literacy and Language Arts* 52 no. 4 Article 5. (Sept/Oct 2013). PDF format.

[106] *Purposeful Interpersonal Interaction in Online Learning: What is it and How is it Measured?*
https://doi.org/10.24059/olj.v24i1.2002
Mehall, Scott. (2020). *Online Learning* 24 no. 1 (March 2020):182–204. PDF format. Available under Creative Common license: CC by 4.0.

[107] *Blended Workplace Learning: The Value of Human Interaction*
https://doi.org/10.1108/ET-01-2017-0004
Hewett, Sunita, Karen Becker, and Adelle Bish. *Education + Training* 61 no. 1 (2019):2–16. Requires subscription or purchase.

Knowledge Transfer by Jamye Sagan

[108] *Knowledge Transfer*
https://trainingindustry.com/wiki/content-development/knowledge-transfer/
Training Industry. (2013). Overall definition of knowledge transfer.

[109] *8 Types of Knowledge Transfer*
https://simplicable.com/new/knowledge-transfer
Spacey, John. (2018). Simplicable. Great description of various methods of knowledge transfer.

Learner Preference by Cindy Plunkett

[110] *Why Learning Preferences Are More Important Than Learning Styles*
https://www.bizlibrary.com/blog/learning-methods/learning-preferences-versus-learning-styles/
Miller, Caroline. (2021). Biz Library blog.

[111] *Learning Styles vs. Learning Preferences: What You Need to Know to Help Your Learner*
https://www.wtmacademy.com/learning-styles-vs-learning-preferences/
Well-Trained Mind Academy.

[112] *Learning Styles: Concepts and Evidence*
https://journals.sagepub.com/doi/full/10.1111/j.1539-6053.2009.01038.x
Pashler, H., McDaniel, M., Rohrer, D., and Bjork, R. (2008). *Psychological Science in the Public Interest*, 9(3), 105–119.

Learning Content Standards by Adam Weisblatt

[113] *Ohio's Learning Standards*
https://education.ohio.gov/Topics/Learning-in-Ohio/Ohios-Learning-Standards/Ohio-Learning-Standards-Resources/Ohio-Learning-Standards-Terminology
Ohio Department of Education. Defines several different types of educational standards.

[114] *CA Department of Education Content Standards*
https://www.cde.ca.gov/be/st/ss/
California State Board of Education. Describes content standards adopted by the California State Board of Education.

[115] *Content Standards*
http://www.ibe.unesco.org/en/glossary-curriculum-terminology/c/content-standards
International Bureau of Education (UNESCO). A definition of content standards.

[116] *What is the Experience API?*
https://xapi.com/overview/
xAPI.com.

[117] *Learning Experience Platforms: The Ultimate LXP Guide for 2022*
https://learn.filtered.com/lxp-guide
filtered. Defines LXP and Discusses their history.

Learning Ecosystem by Catherine Lombardozzi

[118] *Learning Ecosystem: Why You Need One, How to Build It*
https://www.td.org/insights/learning-ecosystem-why-you-need-one-now-and-how-to-build-it
Theodotou, Marina. (December 2020). Association for Talent Development (ATD) blog.

[119] *Your Organization Needs a Learning Ecosystem*
https://hbr.org/2019/07/your-organization-needs-a-learning-ecosystem
Johnson, Whitney. (July 2019). Behind paywall that allows limited free access (two articles per month).

[120] *The 5 Most Important Capabilities for Your Learning Ecosystem*
https://blog.degreed.com/5-important-capabilities-learning-ecosystem/
Danzl, Sarah. (February 2020). Degreed Blog.

[121] *Learning Environments by Design*
Lombardozzi, Catherine. (2020). Association for Talent Development.
ISBN: 978-1562869977.

Learning Environment Modeling (LEM) by Bucky Dodd

[122] *Learning Environment Modeling: Discover a New Solution for Designing World-Class Learning Experiences*
https://lxstudio.com/lem/
LX Studio. An description of the LX Studio Learning Environment Modeling system.

[123] *Overview of Learning Environment Modeling Language (LEML)*
https://www.youtube.com/watch?v=ltn5qrHgbgw
Dodd, Bucky. (2015). YouTube video.

Learning Experience (LX) Design by Jessica Knott

[124] *Increasing Sales Through E-Learning*
https://trainingindustry.com/articles/sales/increasing-sales-through-e-learning/
Hoke, C. (July 2011). Training Industry.

[125] *Quantifying the user experience: Practical statistics for user research*
Sauro, Jeff, and James R. Lewis. (2016). Second edition. Morgan Kaufmann. ISBN: 978-0128023082

[126] *Foundations and definition*
Schumacher, Robert M. (2010). in Handbook of Global User Research, edited by Robert M. Schumacher, 1-20. Morgan Kaufmann. ISBN: 978-0123748522.

[127] *What is learning experience design?*
https://lxd.org/fundamentals-of-learning-experience-design/what-is-learning-experience-design/
Website and video that defines and describes learning experience design.

Learning Management System (LMS) by Phily Hayes

[128] *The Future of the LMS*
https://trainingmag.com/the-future-of-the-lms/
Freifeld, Lorri (2020). Training Magazine.

[129] *Contact North Webinar: The Future of Learning Management Systems*
https://philonedtech.com/contact-north-webinar-the-future-of-learning-management-systems/
Hill, Phil. (2020). Phil on EdTech.

[130] *Reimagining the LMS*
https://www.insidehighered.com/blogs/higher-ed-gamma/reimagining-lms/
Mintz, Steven. (2021). Inside Higher Ed. On a website that allows 5 free articles per month.

Learning Objectives by Julie Dirksen

[131] *New Taxonomy for Learning Objectives*
https://www.worklearning.com/2006/06/01/new_taxonomy_fo/
Thalheimer, Will. (2006). Work-Learning Research, Inc. Blog post.

[132] *Learning Objectives —A Research-Inspired Odyssey*
https://www.worklearning.com/2015/01/29/video-on-lobjs/
Thalheimer, Will. (2015). Work-Learning Research, Inc. Video on what the research says about learning objectives.

[133] *Design for How People Learn, 2nd edition.*
https://usablelearning.com/the-book/
Dirksen, Julie. (2015). New Riders. ISBN: 978-0-13-421128-2.

Machine Learning by W. Duncan Welder IV

[134] *Machine Learning*
https://www.ibm.com/cloud/learn/machine-learning
IBM Cloud Education. (July 2020). An introduction to machine learning, including an overview of history, definitions, applications, and concerns.

Makerspace by Donna Marie Andress

[135] *What is a makerspace?*
https://www.makerspaces.com/what-is-a-makerspace/
An academic perspective on makerspaces with a great overview and introduction to what a Makerspace is. Includes playbooks and project ideas.

[136] *Makerspace*
https://makerspaces.make.co/
This site has a Makerspace directory and links to Make magazine, Maker Faire events, and Maker Shed kits you can buy to create innovative tech-based materials.

Microlearning by Karin Rex

[137] *Micro-learning overview interview with Ray Jimenez*
https://youtu.be/pSxJr6j3O7Y
Jones, Bryan. (2018). eLearningArt. YouTube video.

[138] *How long is microlearning?*
https://axonify.com/blog/how-long-is-microlearning/
Dillon, JD. (2018). Axonify.

[139] *What Is Microlearning: A Complete Guide For Beginners*
https://elearningindustry.com/what-is-microlearning-benefits-best-practices
Andriotis, Nikos. (2018). eLearning Industry.

Online Learning by Jennifer Mathes

[140] *Online Learning for Beginners*
https://www.tonybates.ca/2016/07/15/online-learning-for-beginners-1-what-is-online-learning/
Bates, Tony. (2016). First in a series of ten blog posts about online learning.

[141] *Updated eLearning Definitions*
https://onlinelearningconsortium.org/updated-e-learning-definitions-2/
Sener, John. (2015). Online Learning Consortium.

[142] *How Many Ways Can We Define Online Learning? A Systematic Literature Review of Definitions of Online Learning (1988-2018)*
https://doi.org/10.1080/08923647.2019.1663082
Singh, Vandana, and Alexander Thurman. *American Journal of Distance Education* 33, no. 4 (2019):289–306. Article available for purchase or with a subscription.

[143] *Predictors for Student Success in Online Education*
https://www.ideals.illinois.edu/handle/2142/79736
Mathes, Jennifer Lynn. (2003). PhD Dissertation, University of Illinois at Urbana-Champaign.

Open Educational Resources (OER) by Mark McBride

[144] *Open Educational Resources (OER): Overview and Definition*
https://www.edweek.org/teaching-learning/open-educational-resources-oer-overview-and-definition/2017/04
Sparks, Sarah D. (2017). Education Week.

[145] *The SUNY OER Community Course Experience*
https://online.suny.edu/sunyoercommunitycourse/
State University of New York OER Services. A set of online courses that introduce open educational resources.

[146] *Open Education*
https://hewlett.org/strategy/open-education/
William and Flora Hewlett Foundation. Defines open education and describes the foundation's activities in that area.

[147] *A Basic guide to open educational resources (OER)*
https://unesdoc.unesco.org/ark:/48223/pf0000215804
Butcher, Neil, Asha Kanwar, Stamenda Uvalic-Trumbic. (2015). UNESDOC. Full text available at site.

[148] *OER Commons*
https://www.oercommons.org/
OER Commons is a public digital library of open educational resources.

Pedagogy by Angela Gunder

[149] *Pedagogy A definitive guide to learning practices*
https://resourced.prometheanworld.com/pedagogy-learning-practices/
ResourcEd blog.

[150] *Pedagogy Matters: Standards for Effective Teaching Practice*
https://resourced.prometheanworld.com/pedagogy-learning-practices/
Dalton, Stephanie Stoll. (1998). Center for Research on Education, Diversity and Excellence. University of California Berkeley.

[151] *Pedagogy and Course Design Need to Change. Here's How*
https://www.insidehighered.com/blogs/higher-ed-gamma/pedagogy-
and-course-design-need-change-here%E2%80%99s-how
Mintz, Steven. (2020). Inside Higher Ed. On site that allows 5 free articles
per month.

[152] *What is Pedagogy? Why it's important for teachers to consider*
https://medium.com/educate-pub/what-is-pedagogy-5b2381222418
Brown, John. (2019). Medium, Educate.

Personalized Learning by Ragini Lall

[153] *3 Dimensions of Personalized Learning*
https://www.edutopia.org/article/3-dimensions-personalized-learning
France, Paul Emerich. (2021). George Lucas Educational Foundation.

[154] *The Future of Learning? Well, It's Personal*
https://www.npr.org/2018/11/16/657895964/the-future-of-learning-well-
it-s-personal
Kamenetz, Anya, Robbie Feinberg, and Kyla Calvert Mason. (2018). All
Things Considered, National Public Radio. Audio with transcript.

Predictive Learning Analytics by Ken Phillips

[155] *Evaluate Learning With Predictive Learning Analytics*
https://www.td.org/td-at-work/evaluate-learning-with-predictive-
learning-analytics
Phillips, Ken. (2020). Requires subscription or purchase.

[156] *Predictive Analytics: What it is and why it matters*
https://www.sas.com/en_us/insights/analytics/predictive-analytics.html
SAS Insights. A history of predictive analytics and a description of why
it is important.

[157] *What is predictive analytics?*
https://www.ibm.com/topics/predictive-analytics
IBM. Defines the term and links to a presentation that goes into more
detail.

[158] *2019 State of the Industry: Talent Development Benchmarks and Trends*
https://www.td.org/research-reports/2019-state-of-the-industry
Association for Talent Development (ATD). Requires subscription or
purchase.

Problem-Based Learning (PBL) by Ann Musgrove

[159] *Problem-Based Learning: An Overview of its Process and Impact on Learning*
https://www.sciencedirect.com/science/article/pii/S2452301116300062
Yew, Elaine H.J., and Karen Goh. *Health Professions Education* 2 no. 2 (2016):75–79.

[160] *Problem-based Learning: Case Studies, Experience and Practice*
https://eric.ed.gov/?id=ED450643
Schwartz, Peter, Stewart Mennin, and Graham Webb, eds. (2001). Routledge. ISBN: 978-0749434922.

[161] *Successful Project-Based Learning*
https://hbsp.harvard.edu/inspiring-minds/successful-project-based-learning
Albert, Terri C. (May 22, 2019). Harvard Business Publishing.

Scaffolding by Jennifer Staley

[162] *Instructional Scaffolding in Online Education: What is it and How to do it Right?*
https://corp.kaltura.com/blog/instructional-scaffolding-in-online-education/
Swibel, Danny. (Feb 2019, updated Nov. 2021). Newrow Blog.

[163] *Scaffolding for Online Learning Environments: Instructional Design Strategies that Provide Online Learner Support*
http://www.jstor.org/stable/44428859
Schutt, Maria. *Educational Technology* 43 no. 6 (Nov–Dec 2003):28–35. Requires subscription or purchase.

[164] *The Importance of Instructional Scaffolding*
https://www.teachermagazine.com/au_en/articles/the-importance-of-instructional-scaffolding
Castagno-Dysart, Dawn, Bryan Matera, and Joel Traver. Teacher Magazine. April, 2019.

Simulation by Neal Rowland

[165] *Interactive Simulations for Science and Math*
https://phet.colorado.edu/
Site that contains hundreds of freely available science and math simulations. Based on open-source software.

Social and Informal Learning by Jane Bozarth

[166] *Social And Informal Learning Explained: Why Technology Matters*
https://elearningindustry.com/social-and-informal-learning-explained-technology-matters
Chaffe, Sophie, and David Patterson. (Feb 2016). eLearning Industry.

[167] *The Mediating Role of Social Informal Learning in the Relationship Between Learning Climate and Employability*
https://doi.org/10.1108/CDI-09-2020-0234
Crans, Samantha, Maike Gerken, Simon Beausaert, and Mien Segers. *Career Development International* 26 no. 5 (July 2021):678–696. Downloadable PDF.

[168] *Factors that Influence Informal Learning in the Workplace*
https://doi.org/10.1108/13665620810871097
Berg, Shelley A., and Seung Youn (Yonnie) Chyung. *Journal of Workplace Learning* 20 no. 4 (2008):229–244. Requires subscription or institutional login.

Virtual Reality by Niall Campion

[169] *What is virtual reality?*
https://www.vrs.org.uk/virtual-reality/what-is-virtual-reality.html
Virtual Reality Society. (2017).

Contributor Index

Subject Index

G

game aesthetics, 128
game dynamics, 128
game elements, 22, 129
game mechanics, 129
game thinking, 21, 129
game-based learning (gbl), 21, 61–62, 129, 133
gamification, 21–22, 61–62, 129
gamify, 102, 129

H

hackerspace, 129
haptic feedback, 113, 129
head-mounted display, 123, 129
heutagogy, 16, 23–24, 35–36, 125
higher-order thinking levels, 129
human performance improvement, 109–110
human-centered design, 31, 129

I

immersive projection rooms, 124, 130
implicit learning propensity, 130
instructional design, 25–26, 133
interaction, 63–64
intrinsic motivation, 130
item analysis, 130

J

journey maps, 32, 130

K

knowledge management, 53, 130
knowledge transfer, 85–86

L

learner preference, 27–28, 42, 131
learning and development infrastructure, 48, 130
learning campaign, 46, 130
learning content standards, 87–88
learning ecosystem, 65–66

learning environment modeling (lem), 29–30, 127
learning experience (lx) design, 31–32, 52, 129–130, 133–135
learning management system (lms), 38, 46, 68, 88–90, 134
learning objectives, 91–92
learning strategy, 36, 42, 105, 130
learning style, 28, 131
licensure, 96, 99, 131
LIDAR , 113, 131
long-term memory, 51, 131
lower-order thinking levels, 131

M

machine learning, 115–116, 125–127, 136
makerspace, 117–118, 128–129
Massive Open Online Course (MOOC), 70, 131
measurable behaviors, 43, 131
mental structures, 57–58, 131
metacognition, 132
metacognitive learning, 132
micro-credential, 102, 132
microlearning, 33–34, 135
mixed reality, 114, 124, 132
moment of learning need, 46, 132

O

online learning, 67–68
open access, 70, 132
open educational resources (oer), 69–70, 131–132
open pedagogy, 35, 132
operant conditioning, 76, 132

P

pedagogy, 16, 35–36, 58, 127, 130, 132
performance support, 26, 84, 98, 133
personal learning paths, 46, 133
personalized learning, 37–38, 42
personas, 32, 133
portfolio , 133
predictive learning analytics, 119–120, 134–135

Colophon

About the Book

This book was authored in expeDITA, a DITA-based wiki developed by Don Day. Contents were converted to DocBook, and the book was generated using the DocBook XML stylesheets with XML Press customizations and, for the print edition, the RenderX XEP formatter.

With the exception of this colophon and the advertisement at the back of the book, the interior of this book was generated directly from the wiki with no manual intervention.

About the Content Wrangler Content Strategy Book Series

The Content Wrangler Content Strategy Book Series from XML Press provides content professionals with a road map for success. Each volume provides practical advice, best practices, and lessons learned from the most knowledgeable content strategists and technical communicators in the world. Visit the companion website for more information about the series: contentstrategybooks.com.

We are always looking for ideas for new books in the series. If you have any suggestions or would like to propose a book for the series, send email to proposal@xmlpress.net.

About XML Press

XML Press (xmlpress.net) was founded in 2008 to publish content that helps technical communicators be more effective. Our publications support managers, social media practitioners, technical communicators, and content strategists and the engineers who support their efforts.

Our publications are available through most retailers, and discounted pricing is available for volume purchases for educational or promotional use. For more information, send email to orders@xmlpress.net or call us at (970) 231-3624.

www.ingramcontent.com/pod-product-compliance
Lightning Source LLC
Chambersburg PA
CBHW061318220326
41599CB00026B/4940